Teaching Drama

AN APPROACH TO EDUCATIONAL DRAMA IN THE SECONDARY SCHOOL

R. N. PEMBERTON-BILLING

Director of the Octagon Theatre, Bolton

J. D. CLEGG, A.D.B.

Chorley College of Education, Lancashire

UNIVERSITY OF LONDON PRESS LTD

ISBN 0 340 08386 7

First published 1965
Second edition: third impression 1970
Copyright © 1968 R. N. Pemberton-Billing and J. D. Clegg

University of London Press Ltd
St Paul's House, Warwick Lane, London EC4

Printed in Great Britain by
Butler and Tanner Ltd, Frome and London

Contents

Contents

Foreword

One of the significant developments in education during the past twenty years has been the arrival of drama as a subject in its own right. That children can learn about life by enacting it, as well as by drawing it or reading and writing about it, has come to be an acceptable proposition; and the acceptance has, like the arrival of Cizek-inspired art and 'creative writing', helped schools to recognise that they should be concerned with letting children learn about life rather than with filling empty buckets with information. In areas and schools where drama has had a fair trial, it has appeared that the subject has in fact helped children to become articulate and self-reliant, more at peace with themselves and better adjusted to society.

Twenty years is not, perhaps, a long period in the history of a subject; so if, to some of us, progress seems to have been slow, that is because we feel that we have so much to offer that is desperately needed. One obvious reason why growth has not been faster is the general shortage of teachers, which must affect new subjects even more severely than it does established ones. But while we may wait for an adequate flow of drama specialists into the teaching profession, we must make the fullest use of what force there is.

Here lies the great value of this book. Imaginative yet intensely practical, widely ranging and yet systematic, concise yet packed with material, it is exactly what is wanted by students going out from college to their first jobs, and by those teachers who would very much like to 'try some drama at school', but lack the training necessary to enable them to start confidently with some idea of where they are going.

The authors are both young teachers who have hastened to complete their work while they can still remember what it felt like to go on to the floor to meet that first drama class; to give a four-star lesson, try it on the next class and achieve a five-star flop; to wonder why on earth they didn't choose to teach something safe like ——. Moreover they have contended with the self-conscious post-puberty heavyweights, not solely with juniors whom a puff of stimulation sends up into the air, like chickens when the fox lands in the run.

One hopes that with a clear floor-space, a few boxes, a record-player, a simple kit of percussion instruments and the ideas and material offered by this book, many teachers, young and old, will feel armed for tackling an experience which prevents drama teachers from ever (educationally) dying, or—worse than death—having to justify what they do by reference to "The Syllabus".

S. C. EVERNDEN
Principal Lecturer in Drama
Loughborough Training College

Acknowledgments

Throughout this work our inspiration has been Mr. S. C. Evernden, Principal Lecturer in Drama at Loughborough Training College. He it was who originally convinced us of the value of educational drama, since when he has proved a constant source of encouragement and sympathetic understanding. We hope this book does him justice.

Like all other teachers of drama, we must acknowledge our debt to Mr. Peter Slade and his pioneering work in the development of drama in schools. We should also like to thank our many colleagues in various schools who have helped and tolerated us over the past few years. Special thanks are due to Mr. S. C. Western, Headmaster of the Ivanhoe Secondary Modern School and Community College, Ashby-de-la-Zouch, and Mr. Derrick Palmer, formerly Senior English Master, Castle Rock School, Coalville. We are particularly indebted to Mr. Eugene Cooper of Loughborough, for his invaluable advice on records and equipment; he also took many of the photographs.

Finally, we should like to make it clear that not all the examples of practical activities in Section 4 are original. Many have reached us second- or even third-hand, and will doubtless be recognised by some teachers. They have been included because we found them successful.

R. N. PEMBERTON-BILLING   J. D. CLEGG

Illustrations

1 Drama in action

What is a drama lesson like? It can take place in a variety of situations, under various conditions, but always there should be excitement, a feeling that here something vital is happening.

The school is bright and modern, even severe. The foyer presents an air of efficiency. It is quiet, and your footsteps echo on the polished floor. There is a smell of wax polish and detergent, notices hang limply on the far wall—a feeling of unreality, as if a school full of children cannot possibly exist beyond.

Muffled cries, thuds, chatter and the crash of a musical climax disturb the silence. Activity explodes beyond the double glass doors leading to the hall. To open these doors is to find another world, and run the risk of becoming the centre of an exciting situation.

A drama lesson is just ending. The class lines up quietly and begins to file out into the foyer, joining other children already beginning to move to different classes. The empty hall seems vast and gloomy, full of interesting corners and patches of light. The curtains are closed and spotlights cast irregular pools of shiny light on the floor, emphasising the pattern of polished wood blocks. An intense orange light shines in your eyes. It fades to a full glow, and with a clatter the drama teacher jumps from the stage and begins to sort through some records by the gramophone. With a slight movement he signals the next class to come in, and the hall is once more full of children.

They enter excitedly chattering to one another, removing jackets and pullovers as they go, each one finding a safe spot to dump satchels, books and the many things that children always seem to carry with them. The teacher takes little apparent notice, but the children are obviously aware of his presence, and he seems to be summing up the mood of the class while experimenting with brief snatches of music on the gramophone. Some of the class are discussing something important in pairs and small groups. Some are leaping and weaving around the others as if they are casting spells. A small boy in one corner is walking stiffly, like a clockwork toy. A few children make straight for the gramophone and, as they ply the teacher with questions, try to read the name on the record label as it revolves. They admire the sleeve— an arresting picture—it is *The Firebird*.

A loud crash from the gramophone speaker, set high on the wall, temporarily halts most of the class. They turn and look, not at the loudspeaker but at the teacher, who takes this opportunity to give a sharp clap, followed by a gesture which obviously says, "Come and sit down over here". There is a brief jockeying for places, but very quickly the class is in a semi-circle round the steps on one side of the stage. Some lean on the stage, some sit cross-legged, while others lie with their heads propped in their hands. All seem quite relaxed, especially the teacher. From this distance what he says is barely audible, but soon hands shoot up and the children seem to be offering suggestions. A rucksack . . . camera . . . sandwiches . . . primus stove . . . thermos flask . . . At a decisive movement from the teacher the semi-circle disintegrates, and the children are scattered around the hall, some sitting, some lying, some seeking the splashes of light, some preferring the dark corners. A few children perch on the edge of the half-dozen rostrum blocks placed haphazardly about the floor. Stacks of metal chairs line one wall; the occasional child finds a haven near them. The teacher's voice is now quite clear. The whole class is silent as he begins a story: "It is early on a summer's morning. Outside the sun is shining. We are asleep in bed; very soon the alarm clock will sound . . ." The children seem asleep— some restlessly, some deeply. The teacher meanwhile has moved imperceptibly over to the stage, and suddenly he rattles a side-drum, and the class reacts—some quite violently. They seem absorbed in the real process of getting out of bed. Some manage it straight away, some roll over and pull bedclothes over their faces, while others are quite obviously finding cold lino under their bare feet. "Go into the bathroom and have a good wash. Don't forget behind your ears! Clean your teeth and get dressed."

The children's activities begin to vary. Some obviously wash in their pyjamas, while others get partly dressed first. Some make tap noises as they fill their own wash-basins. A general hatred of washing is shown by perfunctory and noisy splashing, but just a few hold their heads under the taps. The narration continues, and the children rush down to breakfast, cut sandwiches and pack things to take for a day in the country.

They set off to catch the bus in a happy mood, whistling, running and skipping. To help them music blares through the loudspeaker: a 'pop' record from the past—*Jumping Bean* —just the thing to convey the spirit of setting off, and the children respond to it well. They meet friends and begin the bus journey, amid much slapstick comedy with imaginary bus conductors.

The transition from one activity to the next is quite natural. The teacher never says things twice, in fact he hardly interrupts the action: the children seem to hear every word without apparently listening. Most of the time they are completely absorbed in what they are doing, and only occasionally, when they need to sort out some snag, do they become conscious of the hall and their neighbours. The hall is transformed every few moments into a fresh location, sometimes by sounds from the gramophone, sometimes simply by the sincerity and absorption with which the children create their own ideas for the story. Moods vary tremendously, and the class is at one moment noisy and lively, at the next quiet and intent.

The only control over mood is by the teacher suggesting where they are and what they are doing, or by the type of sound they can hear. Now, for instance, they are searching for wild flowers and listening for bird songs. 'Morning', from Peer Gynt, sets the quiet atmosphere. They cross a farmyard and feed ducks and dogs, providing their own noises (some of the walkers forsake their walk to become, briefly, a farm dog). They choose a spot, eat their meal, rest and begin to play ball games. An unusual record is used for this—an almost forgotten 'hit'—a clever, twangy, fast guitar piece called Little Rock Getaway. After the games, and a short spell of fishing, everyone goes in for a swim. The children swim with lazy slow strokes to The Swan of Tuonela, covering vast areas of the hall. All sorts of interesting experiments are going on: someone in the corner is trying a backstroke, blowing bubbles as she goes.

Soon the excursion comes to an end, the children pack up their things and head for home—a shower of rain causing mild panic on the way. At last when they are back in bed all is still once more.

Quietly, and only gently breaking the spell, the teacher calls the class to him. In a very different mood from when they came in, the class is again clustered in a semi-circle round the gramophone at the foot of the steps. The children seem relaxed and satisfied. Quiet discussion is taking place now, and it seems to draw naturally to a close with a few of the class getting up and collecting their things, while the teacher returns to re-sort his records. Ties are replaced, blazers and cardigans put on, as the children drift towards the door into what is obviously the routine of forming quiet lines ready to go. The timing was just right, the bell rings and the teacher sees the class out into the foyer.

This is just one example of a drama lesson, and is the sort of work that a first-year class in a secondary school might be doing. If we looked in on a second-year class we might see a market scene in full swing—suddenly an old lady faints or a messenger arrives to announce that the king is on his way. A third-year class might show us small groups clustered round the hall making up their own plays from a given idea, or the whole class working on a dance drama based on the Fire of London. Whatever the activity the first thing that would strike the outside observer would be the atmosphere of sincere absorption.

The sheer magic of the lesson described can really occur —sometimes! It can have as profound an effect upon the teacher as it does on the children. Only when he has experienced it will the teacher begin to realise what drama is all about. No amount of reading or argument will convince him that this sort of work is possible. He must try it for himself. We hope that this book will at least give him enough confidence to start.

Even the experienced drama teacher, in the best of situations, will have only a limited number of completely successful lessons. Unless he is prepared to accept this he will quickly become frustrated. Even the simplest things can upset well-laid plans: a hot sultry afternoon will not be the best time to be exploring in the arctic; the most willing class, that has just been severely 'squashed' because of some breach of discipline elsewhere in the school, will not be in the most receptive mood. Again, many schools will not have a modern hall equipped with curtains and spotlights, and the teacher must work harder to create his atmosphere (see Section 6, page 129). This is not an insuperable difficulty as most children, if they are really absorbed, will establish their own atmosphere irrespective of the physical surroundings. Space, however, is vital. Drama as we have described it cannot really come to any full fruition in a class-room. There must be room to move freely. The main essential is enthusiasm, based on a sincere belief that the work has a real educational value. Armed with this, and some understanding of how to approach the work, the teacher prepared to 'have a go' has every chance of success. This book is intended to give such people an understanding of the aims of drama, and suggest ways in which they may be achieved.

1 Some lean on the stage, some sit cross-legged . . .

2 The children seem asleep—some restlessly, some deeply.

3 'Go into the bathroom and have a good wash. Don't forget behind your ears! Clean your teeth and get dressed.'

4 The girls take a last look at themselves in the mirror before setting off.

5 They set off to catch the bus in a happy mood, running and skipping.

6 They cross a farmyard where there are animals to stroke.

7 Some find chickens to feed.

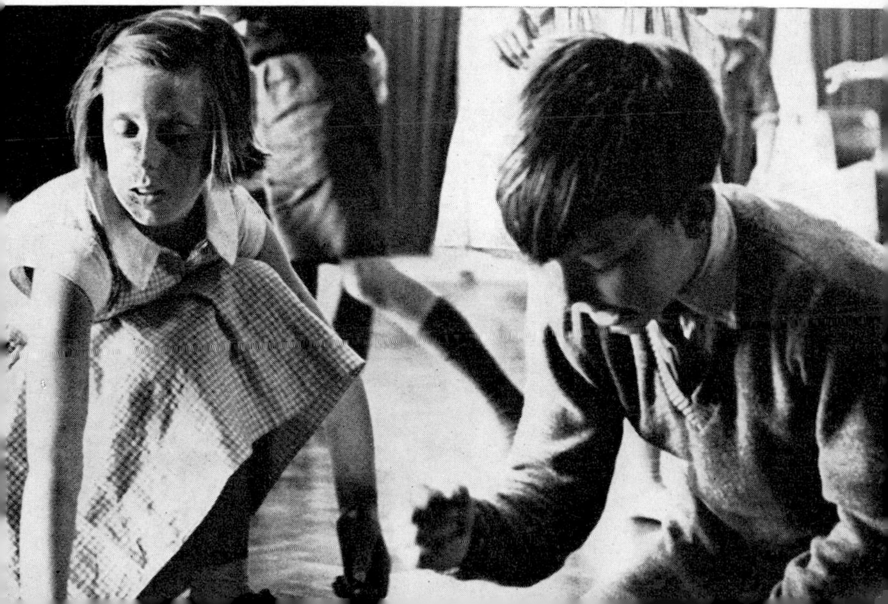

8 They choose a picnic spot and have a drink from their thermos flasks.

9 . . . and begin to play ball games.

2 Drama and its aims

We have seen a drama lesson in action, and sensed something of the atmosphere that surrounds it. It is this atmosphere that tends to make many people suspicious, and feel that the drama teacher is offering the children an emotional mud-bath in which to wallow. Is there, in fact, any value in drama, other than providing an enjoyable but somewhat chaotic activity that fits in with ideas of 'freedom' and 'the modern approach' to education? To answer this question we must decide what drama is and, in the light of our definition, what it has to offer.

Child drama is a creative activity and, as such, fulfils the normal function of all creative activity; it provides a medium through which the individual can express his ideas—his re-actions to the impressions he receives—and, by expressing them, learn to evaluate them. By this process, vague impressions are brought into sharp focus, puzzling impressions are understood, fragmentary ones are completed and alarming ones are faced so that fear is overcome. This use of the creative arts makes us examine what we are thinking and feeling. Imaginative observation is stimulated and our understanding of ourselves and the world around us is extended and deepened.

So, because it is one of the creative arts, child drama begins, not with somebody's text, but with the child's self-expression through the acting of his own experiences. Child drama is

B

10 The children pack up their things, and head for home.

not theatre. All too frequently drama in schools is a diluted version of adult theatre, conducted as if the aim were to train actors for the stage. Acting involves the use of techniques developed for the sole purpose of communicating with an audience, and requires the actor to bring to life ideas and conflicts for the benefit, not of himself, but of his audience.

In the initial stages of rehearsal the actor may well be genuinely involved in these ideas and conflicts, but the requirements of theatre and the presence of an audience will usually modify and alter what he would like to do, and how he would like to do it. Theatre is an art for showing. In order, for example, to let the audience hear and see, the actor's speech must be louder and his movements larger than in real life; and to make the loud speech and the enlarged movements seem natural, techniques have to be learnt—techniques so difficult that comparatively few amateur actors master them. The theatre thus imposes severe limitations on self-expression, and to these are added the requirements of the script and the producer.

Faced with lines to be read or recited, movements to be remembered and the need for effective projection, the child actor can make little use of his own observations of life, his own speech and movement, or his own way of reacting to situations. He becomes an automaton in the hands of the producer, giving little of his real self to the part, and learning little about the real life which—it is to be hoped—lies behind the chosen script. (All that he learns is to imitate adult actors acting—a lesson of little value whether the aim be the primary one of using drama as a means of learning about life, or the secondary one of giving the child an experience which will eventually lead him to fresh, vital and natural acting.)

In child drama theatrical limitations do not exist. The child is free to develop ideas and conflicts along his own lines, and reach his own conclusions. If, for example, the child is asked to explore a situation where he, as a teenage son, arrives home at one o'clock in the morning to find an irate father waiting up for him, he is able, by drawing upon his observations of life, to develop and resolve the situation in his own way, using his natural speech and movement. He has, in fact, elucidated his ideas by the sincere expression of them, without being limited by any techniques for showing which would tend to inhibit his true reactions. It is only through such sincerity and absorption that true creative work becomes possible.

This is not to say that theatre is either bad or wrong, but merely that it should not be confused with child drama. Theatre can be a useful and enjoyable out-of-school activity: child drama is an educational medium.

From the very earliest days drama has fulfilled a basic need in man. It has enabled him to come to terms with himself and his environment. In the normal topocosm of primitive man, the basic problem of food, i.e., the need for a good harvest, was ever-present. He would, therefore, identify himself with a flourishing wheat crop by evolving a leaping dance to represent the growth of the wheat in an effort to understand and influence it. This is drama. In fact the word itself comes from the Greek word 'dromenon' meaning 'a thing done'.

In a modern context drama can still perform this function for the child. He is the one for whom it has the greatest value, the one who still has many of the fears of primitive man, and needs some piece of magic to explain or allay them. If he is afraid of being in the dark he can try to comfort himself by peopling his darkness with imaginary friendly characters.

In our society the child is the one who has the least control over his environment and destiny, and is dependent solely upon adult decisions. He has a desperate need for magic and invention to help him understand his surroundings, and make them bearable; his own secure world can so easily be shattered by the simple necessities of adult life. The normal happy child with his circle of friends and familiar things may suddenly be uprooted when father moves to another job many miles away. To compensate for this violent loss of security he must temporarily invent his own world, until he has readjusted himself.

His magic may often simply be in order to escape from imposed adult conventions with which he cannot cope. The child who is afraid of school invents illness to keep him at home. In these situations drama can still help. Where the magic is a worthwhile thing and obviously helps the child, drama can help him to invent more successfully; where the magic is not necessarily desirable, as in the example about school, drama can help him to cope with the problem, by letting him do plays about school in which he will come to realise that school need not necessarily be unpleasant. In this way he can work out not only what his problem is, but also possible ways of solving it.

Children are naturally conscious of the need to invent and, through this, discover. In their own play they dramatise without adult help, experimenting with life and death through 'cowboys and Indians', and experiencing power by becoming the 'king of the castle'.

Through this play the child learns to grow up. He comes to grips gradually with the real world. He can explore impending situations and so become less afraid of them. In playing at 'schools'—before he actually goes to school—he discovers how he feels, and adjusts himself to the idea of school before being suddenly plunged into it.

Having discovered the world as it exists, and begun to come to terms with it, he starts to experiment with what he considers to be the added freedom enjoyed by the adults who control his world. He tries to experience this control, and through it influence the course of events. If he desperately wants a bicycle he may play 'mothers and fathers', taking the part of the father and giving himself the bicycle.

In time he learns that being an adult is not as easy as he thought; he begins to realise that added freedom means added responsibility. The wider the choice of decisions the more difficult it is to make the right one. The important thing is that the child, in his drama, can make a decision; he can make it because he is not afraid of making the wrong one, since nothing dreadful will happen if he does. With the teacher or a sympathetic adult to guide him, he can reconsider his decisions, and perhaps begin again.

The drama teacher's job is to discipline and direct the child's play into channels where he needs to make worthwhile decisions and discoveries. An aimless story of 'mothers and fathers' could be developed into one where important family decisions must be made. Drama then becomes a positive educational force, not merely a useful but haphazard way of learning. It also provides a link between the more tightly supervised aspects of school work, and the completely unsupervised play of the child. The child can enjoy himself playing at fishing in a pond; by directing this play, i.e., asking him to fish for particular specimens, the teacher can harness play to learning. Thus, the child will begin to realise that learning can be an enjoyable process.

Accepting that drama is, in general, a valuable educational force, we still need—if we are to teach the subject with a full sense of purpose—to examine the specific benefits that it can afford children. The aspects considered in the following pages are not arranged in any particular order and, of course, there is much overlapping.

SELF-EXPRESSION

The child is continually gathering impressions and facts about himself and the world around him. It is only by expressing how he feels about these impressions and facts that he will be able to sort them out for himself, to clarify, understand and develop them. In this way they are related to life and assume real meaning. In drama the child is able to express his feelings about various things and, with the help of the teacher, reconsider and adjust them. For example, in a scene in which he is a policeman he may feel he has to drag everyone off to prison. By discussing the scene afterwards, he can begin to form a more mature judgement. The child must be given every opportunity for self-expression throughout his development. If not he will find himself trying to relate new impressions and facts to ones not yet properly digested or understood.

Today the child spends so much time watching television,

going to the pictures, or sitting in a classroom absorbing facts, that he is in danger of losing the chance of expression through normal play. Drama can help to overcome this danger.

IMAGINATIVE DEVELOPMENT

Imagination, to many people, means the ability to conjure strange fantasies in one's mind; the more unlikely the invention the more 'imagination' it is supposed to show.

Imagination can deal with fantasy, but for most of us it involves something more down-to-earth—the ability to re-arrange our store of experiences and images into new ideas. We can for example conjure up pleasant pictures of future holidays by drawing upon this store. Our conceptions of Spain might be based upon such things as a poster once seen of a bullfight, a Spanish dance performed in a school play, and a particularly hot day spent on the beach at Blackpool.

In drama, imaginative work usually involves trying to transfer oneself to another situation, or to identify oneself with another person. The value of this 'mental mobility' is that it helps towards a sympathetic understanding of how other people live and feel. It increases awareness and sensitivity, and is the essence of human contact in everyday life. How much offence is given, how many strikes are caused, not through maliciousness, but through an inability to imagine not only how the other person feels, but also the possible consequences of the contemplated action? Likewise there is value, in thinking through drama, of the plight of the refugee, the real meaning of hunger or, on a more immediate level, realising how parents must feel

when a thoughtless child arrives home later than he was expected.

Less obviously, there is a desperate need for younger adolescents to be able to envisage and prepare for life after the age of twenty; so many cannot imagine any life other than that of a teenager. Drama can help them to explore and foresee as many alternatives as possible, and realise that the dream world of romance is not borne out in the experience of most people.

The advantage of drama over many other media is that the child has the opportunity of using his imagination to the full, without being restricted by too many technicalities; he can say what he feels about things without being hampered by, for instance, poor spelling or grammar. Under these conditions the power to imagine has the opportunity to grow and develop, and will inevitably influence all other aspects of school work.

MOVEMENT

Throughout his growth the child is continually wrestling with the problem of physical readjustment. If, for example, he outgrows his strength, he may feel self-conscious about his movements and inhibit them. The teenager frequently lacks confidence in movement simply because he is constantly coming face-to-face with new situations in which he just does not know how to move. Does the young man introduced to his new employer shake hands with him or not? If he does not know, he may solve the problem by stuffing his hands into his pockets, creating a false impression of loutishness.

The child must also learn to share space; to realise that other people are entitled to move freely, and to respect their right to do so. In a crowded corridor he must be prepared to adjust and control his movement to meet the situation, and not just barge through.

Drama can help in two ways. Firstly it can give a child the chance to loosen up his movement generally, to become aware of space, and to discover various ways in which it is possible to move—walking a tight-rope or being a blind man feeling his way round a strange room. Secondly, by placing him in a wide variety of situations, drama can foster confidence through discovering, discussing and practising appropriate ways in which to move—bowing to a king or entering the boss's office.

Increased confidence will enable the child to experience the possibilities of self-expression through movement: he will feel a new sense of physical freedom. This, in turn, will open up a fresh world of feeling for him; a world which he would be unlikely to have discovered through the limited demands of everyday movements.

SPEECH

Speech is the most common means of communication, but if it is to be used to its fullest advantage the speaker must be able to make sympathetic contact with his audience: he must genuinely communicate. Isolated 'exercises for speaking' are of limited value, except for specific remedial work. If any real value is to be gained, speech must stem from a genuine desire to express feelings and thought.

Fluency, or speech flow, is usually the initial problem: the ability not only to convert thoughts and ideas into words, but also to string them together and relate them. Drama deals with this problem by presenting the child with situations in which he is called upon to communicate a wide selection of thoughts and ideas. This may be through speech work in pairs—a policeman directing a stranger, or a fast-talking salesman trying to sell a vacuum cleaner to a reluctant housewife—or later through discussions and story-making.

If words are to have any real effect they must be spoken in a vital and interesting manner. Ideas are conveyed more by variations in pitch, pace and emphasis than by literal dictionary meaning. Usually it is through intonation that subtlety of meaning is communicated. The opportunities to experiment with and extend the vocal range are limited in everyday life. Drama should include speech situations which are as varied as possible—shouting instructions across a river on a windy day, whispering important directions to fellow captives without waking a sleeping guard, or trying to convince a pawnbroker that your watch is really gold.

To be effective speech must be controlled. It is, therefore, necessary for the speaker to be able to control the emotional reaction prompting the speech. Too much excitement while delivering an urgent message may result not only in nobody understanding it, but also in the delivery of the wrong message.

Speech work will be wasted if, in the end, the child cannot easily be heard. He must be made aware of the importance of clarity. The point can be brought home by the use of situations needing clear speech: an enemy agent passing a difficult verbal message to a colleague on a busy railway station, or a shop assistant explaining to a rather deaf old lady just how a washing machine works.

The great advantage of approaching speech work through drama is that the speech results from a genuine involvement in situations in which there is real human contact. This stimulates a sincere attempt at communication.

ORGANISING IDEAS

The development of the imagination will result in a flow of ideas. If full value is to be obtained from these ideas, the child must learn to organise them into a recognisable shape. He may have all sorts of exciting and imaginative ideas for a story, but unless he has the ability to sort out and relate them they will be wasted.

Drama gives the child the opportunity to practise and improve his ability to organise his ideas. The construction of a 'group play', if it is to succeed, demands a genuine understanding of dramatic shape and climax: an understanding that emerges from being faced with the practical problems involved. This practical approach leads to a deeper appreciation of the construction of plays and stories than does any artificial analysis.

LEARNING TO LISTEN

Most people tend to ignore sound in self-defence, being as they are inundated with it from motor-cars, factories, television sets, radios, aeroplanes, etc. At times it may be necessary to do this to preserve one's sanity: the danger lies in becoming immune to sound.

The ability to interpret sound sensitively is essential if we are to appreciate the world around us. We cannot hope to understand the more subtle meanings of a speaker's words unless we can interpret the inflections and variations of pitch he uses to convey them. Close listening is also a valuable lesson in concentration, and children usually enjoy such situations as creeping through an imaginary wood, listening for the snap of a twig under the foot of a suspicious game-keeper. Once they can listen closely to simple sounds, they can begin to listen to music. They might, for example, be asked to pick out the climax in a piece of music and then to utilise it in a play or dance drama. Indeed, much incidental music teaching can be achieved during drama lessons.

'PLAYING-OUT'

In encouraging truth and sincerity the teacher must be prepared for the results to be occasionally unpalatable: they must be accepted as valid creative work, although it should not in any way be suggested that the attitudes to life shown are condoned. Nevertheless, opportunities must be given for 'playing-out' crude notions of life. To ignore or suppress them is to suggest that some creative activities are forbidden by adults. This will produce an inhibited form of creation, restricted by the desire to avoid criticism, and resulting in the frustration of truth and sincerity.

Typical reasons for these undesirable activities are:

Uncertain and immature views of life: believing that the solution to all argument lies in physical violence.

A desire to shock authority: introducing swear-words at every conceivable opportunity.

A sense of inadequacy resulting in the feeling that certain activities—sporting a cosh or getting drunk—will prove one to be more adult.

A general disappointment with the adult world, usually resulting from the inability to appreciate that life, if it is to be worthwhile, requires a positive effort. This often leads to hostility towards the world in general.

A wish to 'let off steam' in an attempt to throw off the restrictions of society—at least for a short time.

Courses of action to deal with these anti-social tendencies will vary, *but the first step must be to create an atmosphere of mutual trust.* Without this children will never discuss what they really feel: they are very adept at producing the sort of responses they sense will be most acceptable.

When children first start working in groups and making plays they usually see this as a wonderful opportunity to do all the things reserved for the adult world. Their conception of this world is one in which people have complete freedom and licence to do as they wish.

The best way of correcting these misconceptions is by discussion after the plays in which they have occurred, e.g., "Would it not be better to have a reasonable discussion with your neighbour about his noisy parties, rather than going next door and hitting him?"

The desire to shock authority will probably lose its savour if the teacher refuses to be shocked, and is prepared to recognise and, if necessary, discuss these 'shocking' activities in the normal course of events.

Anti-social tendencies resulting from a sense of inadequacy can be dealt with by giving the child the opportunity to 'be' and 'do' the things which to him represent adulthood, so that the fallacy of his conceptions becomes apparent: he will 'play out' the tendencies. The boy with the cosh is shown up to be a thoughtless bully: a cosh does not make an adult.

It is an accepted fact that it is healthy to let off steam when angry or frustrated. If this can take place in a drama lesson, and correspond as closely as possible to the action the child would like to take in reality, its pointlessness should become apparent, perhaps through repetition in the polishing of an improvised play in which the action takes place. The throwing of a stone through an unpleasant neighbour's window is much better done in pretence in drama than with a real stone in actuality. There is now ample evidence to show that enacting the deed in pretence reduces the impulse to do it in reality.

The 'playing-out' of these crude notions should lead to a realisation of their inadequacy, and stimulate the desire to replace them with something better. The teacher must obviously at this stage have a concrete alternative, as this is one of the occasions when adult advice will be readily accepted.

It must be made quite clear at this point that the solving of genuine problems, which occur quite naturally in the course of the child's drama, is a very different thing from actually encouraging the problems to occur.

The former is a healthy approach, the latter dangerous, and best left to the psychiatrist, as should be the genuine psychiatric case. The drama teacher's job is to use drama as an educational medium, and not as a therapy. Any 'drama therapy' should be left to those especially trained in this work.

SOCIAL TRAINING

One of the most important problems that the young adolescent has to face is that of adapting himself to the adult world. Confidence acquired through drama can usefully be employed, and indeed further developed, by discussing, practising and exploring the sort of adult social situation in which the teenager may feel ill at ease. The natural awkwardness that may be felt when ordering a meal in a restaurant, possibly resulting in brash anti-social behaviour, can be considerably reduced by discussing and experiencing similar situations through drama.

The teenager is frequently too embarrassed to admit his ignorance of social procedure and, to hide this, may pretend that it does not concern him. He is then forced to develop his own code of behaviour, which is often unacceptable and usually anti-social. It is the drama teacher's responsibility to ensure that specific problems of social behaviour do arise. Once the child has been made conscious of his own obligations to society it is possible to discuss society's obligations to him as an individual. There is scope here for work on such public services as the Police Force (the policeman's job is to assist the public as well as to uphold the law!), or the various activities of his local council, for which the teenager will soon share responsibility as a ratepayer and voter.

TOLERANCE

A tolerant attitude towards other people can only be achieved through an understanding of the emotional effects that the problems of life have on them. Such an understanding can arise from a genuine experience of similar problems, but it can also arise through the effort to identify oneself with another person, and the recognition of how they are feeling. By placing the child in suitable situations drama can extend the range of his emotional experiences, thereby helping him to realise, through the process of identification, the impact of a wide variety of problems upon different people. It is also possible to explore the effect of several aspects of the same problem. The opportunity of being both the father and the son in a situation involving a difference of opinion between the two encourages an appreciation of both points of view. This type of work can be extended to include the problems of people in authority (social training), such as the cinema manager faced with a queue of unruly teenagers.

ARTISTIC AWARENESS

Dramatic work helps to give a greater awareness of the arts generally, in that it offers a first-hand experience and understanding of creative activity. The demand for personal involvement increases sensitivity towards mood, atmosphere and emotional depth.

This greater sensitivity leads to a less superficial appreciation of life. In art, for example, it should stimulate a desire to paint not only what is seen but also what is felt. Consequently it may be realised that a painting can be more than merely representational, or indeed that it need not be even that. Similarly in literature more than the basic story can be appreciated. The real point here is that an increased artistic awareness will enable a child to lead a richer, more complete life.

DISCIPLINE

If discipline is always imposed from outside the child will never really learn to live. He will not always have a teacher or parent watching to see that things are done properly. If he is to achieve any success in later life he must learn and practise self-discipline.

Drama not only helps the child to control himself for his own benefit, but what is more important, helps him to control his reactions when he needs to be with, or work with, other people. As drama usually consists of class or group activities the individual must learn to discipline himself and, when necessary, subordinate his own feelings to those of the group. This ability to realise how the rest of the group feels, and act accordingly, is called 'group sensitivity' and the cultivation of it forms an important part of the work.

Self-discipline can only be learnt if children are given the chance to practise it. A certain amount of freedom must, therefore, be allowed. A class that is always closely watched and supervised will never know how to behave if left to its own devices. The danger of continual supervision is that the association of "I am being watched" with "I must behave" may all too easily lead to the opposite assumption—"I am not being watched, therefore I need not behave".

Drama, to some extent, provides scope for learning self-discipline in controlled surroundings. If a class is split into small groups for rehearsals, they cannot all claim constant attention, and will need to work for much of the time on their own initiative. Untrained children too often tend to use freedom for the purposes of destruction. Drama can help them to form the habit of using freedom creatively.

c

INTEGRATION

Drama, by its very nature, embraces most aspects of a child's development. It is possible, by taking advantage of an enthusiastic and vital Drama Department, to integrate dramatic work with the learning processes and content of other subjects. It is difficult to give examples of this without stating the obvious. However, to show that such work needs to be handled with care, it is worth pointing out the difficulties and common fallacies in one popular approach. Children who have been allowed to experience fully the physical and emotional aspects of moments in history will tend to understand more readily the reasons for and the consequences of historical events. But this is very different from trying to teach the facts of history through dramatisation. A play based on the facts will, if our drama course has been successful, inevitably sacrifice historical truth for dramatic shape. This may produce good drama but bad history. The teacher should, therefore, not attempt to teach historical facts through drama, but concentrate rather upon the thoughts and feelings of the people who made history, in an effort to make the child realise that they were as real as he himself is.

The improvement in flow of language and ideas will be an obvious advantage in most school work, particularly in English. In fact drama should be reflected in the general atmosphere of the school, in so far as the children should become more tolerant, interesting and balanced people than they would otherwise have been.

3   Drama in practice

In Section 2 the value and aims of drama as an educational medium have been discussed. How can these aims be achieved in practice?

Drama is a creative subject in which the child expresses himself through the media of speech and movement, in the same way as in art he expresses himself through form and colour and in composition through the written word. The child excited by a visit to a coal-mine will want to express his excitement. He may simply talk about it, but if he finds that words are inadequate, he may paint a picture, write a story, or make up a play about it. He expresses himself through one of these arts.

In drama the work is based on the child's natural desire to express himself through play and make-believe; and if his views are to be expressed sincerely—which they must be if the work is to have real value—they must not be hampered by the technicalities of theatre. The child can express his own views only through his own plays or improvisations. For this reason work is not based on scripts or concerned with performing to an audience. The teacher stimulates and suggests activities, but the children respond with their own interpretations. Moreover, they work all at the same time, so that no-one is watching. In this way self-consciousness is avoided, and the child will feel free to express his own views sincerely.

The drama teacher's first aim must be to create an atmosphere in which the children will tackle the work seriously (see Section 6, page 129). Children new to drama will often delight in treating everything as a huge joke, either to cover up their self-consciousness, or from sheer ignorance of how to use the unaccustomed freedom. This problem—so often the stumbling-block for the inexperienced drama teacher—can be overcome quite easily by creating a very definite atmosphere of 'off jackets and let's get down to work', and by using situations likely so to interest the children that they quickly become absorbed in them. It will not take a class of rowdy boys long to become completely absorbed in a movement session based on sword fighting, or any other energetic activity. Once the teacher has stirred their imaginations and captured their interest they will be willing and eager to experiment further. They will gain confidence in the teacher, and through this confidence he will be able to lead them towards more sensitive situations, requiring greater sincerity and absorption; situations which, prematurely presented, would have made them giggle self-consciously, or stand gawking.

When the children realise that drama is an enjoyable activity, but nevertheless one in which they are expected to work hard and seriously, the teacher will have achieved his first aim—an atmosphere in which to work. Where does he go from here?

For practical purposes the work can be divided into three main kinds of activity, which all lead to the improvised play, as shown in Fig. 1.

There is, of course, considerable overlap in the activities, but generally speaking they cover the following features:

1. *Movement.* Covers all aspects of spontaneous movement, from chasing a butterfly to hauling on a rope, or just moving to music (i.e., dance).
2. *Speech.* Covers all forms of improvised oral expression, including conversation, discussion, debates, story-making, speeches and word games.
3. *Movement and speech together.* Covers all situations where the child moves and speaks simultaneously, and leads directly to group improvisations.

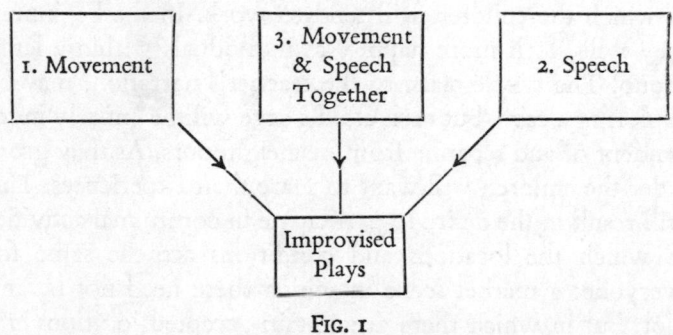

FIG. 1

Throughout this work there are two general lines of progression. Firstly, the development of the child's ability to use his own imagination; and secondly, the development of his ability to work successfully with other people.

The first line of progression starts with the exploration of simple activities presented by the teacher: activities which concern only 'being' something or 'doing' something, and which do not extend to the development of a dramatic situation. For instance, to a narration, children explore a dark sea cave, feeling the shingle under their feet, and smelling the seaweed. As their imagination develops they will be expected to decide for themselves the nature of the cave and what is to be found inside. When they become more used to using their imaginations the teacher will be able to leave more and more decisions to them, until the stage is reached when they are capable of taking on the responsibility for making up their own plays in groups, without his assistance. The teacher then becomes not so much a source of inspiration as a sympathetic critic giving help where necessary.

The second line of progression concerns the changing way in which the children will tend to work. In the beginning they will work more happily as individuals within a large group. The whole class, to the teacher's narration, may be exploring a cave, but each child's cave will be entirely independent of and separate from his neighbours. As they grow older the children will want to share their experiences. This will result in the desire to participate in communal activities in which the locations and conditions are the same for everyone: a market scene in which there need not be any plot, but in which there are certain accepted locations and conventions. The child is now becoming aware of the group in which he is working. When these communal activities take some dramatic shape we have the class play.

If drama is to be soundly based on 'natural' beginnings this type of work must be experienced at some stage of the course. In theory, it should begin in the junior school. In practice, however, regardless of any previous experience, young seniors still work more happily as individuals and in pairs, as if they were, in their drama, retracing and consolidating their social growth in order to move forward more confidently. The next move is towards the group play.

Initially the group play will be based upon the sort of crowd scenes that the children have been doing; after experimenting with various aspects of 'being' and 'doing' things in a market-place, they should be ready to make up small plays about an incident that takes place in a market. They are unlikely, at this stage, to exhibit any real desire to show these plays to the rest of the class.

By the beginning of the third year they should be working quite happily in small self-contained groups.

BREAKING DOWN THE THREE MAIN TYPES OF ACTIVITY INTO
A DETAILED PROGRESSION

We have discussed the aims of drama. The three main types of activity through which these aims are achieved, and the lines along which the work progresses, have been considered. It is now necessary to be more detailed, and break down Fig. 1 (on page 37) into a workable scheme. At first sight such clinical analysis may appear cold-blooded and out of sympathy with the creative approach so essential to the subject. However, some analysis of work is necessary. One of the dangers of drama teaching is to let lessons deteriorate into a series of enjoyable, but rather aimless, activities. The teacher must know where he is going.

In Fig. 3, which can be found facing page 128, the three main types of activity shown in Fig. 1 (page 37) have been divided into progressive steps. Each step is contained in a separate block. The section on the left covers the progression of movement, the section on the right the progression of speech, and the section in the middle the progression of speech and movement together—or improvisation. These sections are obviously closely linked, and should progress simultaneously. Thus, a class that is working on improvised class plays to music, based on the children's own ideas (block 4, page 43—dance drama), might well in another drama lesson be working on speeches, debates and discussions (block 11, page 47), or class plays made up by children from given crowd situations (block 18, page 52). Likewise it is possible to cover some of the speech work in block 11 in a session devoted to block 18, e.g., a general addressing his troops, or a soapbox orator. The suggested progression, in fact, concerns the *emphasis* of lessons at various stages, rather than any strict chronology.

Without losing sight of these links we shall, for the sake of simplicity, take each block separately. (Suggested activities to cover the kind of work in each block will be found in Section 4, pages 68 to 125.)

BLOCKS 1-6   Movement

In drama, the general aims of all movement work are firstly to increase the awareness of space, secondly to give the opportunity of exploring the vast range of movement possible within this space, and thirdly to encourage an interpretation of ideas in terms of movement. All movement, however controlled, should be stimulated by emotions; e.g., "Because I *am* a witch, I shall find myself moving like one", rather than "If I move like this, I shall *look* like a witch". The former is '*being* and *doing*', which is valuable and creative, the latter is '*appearing* to be, for the sake of *showing*', which is insincere, and therefore false. A vocabulary of movement should be built up, not by learning suggested movements to fit various situations, but by creating movements as a result of personal feelings. When the child has gained confidence and control over his movements, he should be in a position to contribute to group movement.

MIME

The use of the word 'mime' has been deliberately avoided in the section on movement because it implies a highly specialised and exact art form, where everything is interpreted through movement at the expense of speech. As much drama work is aimed at encouraging speech, to inhibit it deliberately would appear to be a retrograde step.

Although movement without speech will, in some ways, be more expressive than movement which accompanies speech, the teacher is more concerned with making use of the child's natural abilities, than in establishing any fresh conventions. The role of drama is to develop the child as a person, not as a performer. Therefore, throughout movement work the child should be allowed to speak if and when he feels the need.

BLOCK I — *Stimulation and control of movement*

All movement work, both now and later, will gain immeasurably if it is preceded by some form of relaxation. This enables both the body and mind to concentrate entirely on the work in hand.

The child should be introduced to the drama course through movement, in order to loosen him physically.

Spontaneous and creative movement will lead to spontaneous and creative speech.

However, before movement can be used as a means of self-expression, he must learn that physical responses to the emotions must be controlled. This requires practice, and is best achieved by presenting varied emotional situations requiring different physical responses. In the beginning only the clearest differentials should be attempted, e.g., the difference between slow and fast, light and heavy, etc. *Avoid suggesting to the child that he must move softly because he is a burglar; aim rather at so absorbing the child in being a burglar that he moves softly quite naturally.* Control, then, is not artificially imposed by the teacher, but comes through the material he uses.

BLOCK 2 — *Imaginative movement, individually and in pairs and groups—teacher's stimulation*

Once the child has gained confidence and control in his movement as an individual, he will be ready and indeed eager to work with other children, either in pairs or in small groups. Teacher stimulation is still predominant, but the sounds and situations used to stimulate movement can be more complex, suggesting such things as climax and anticlimax. By this time some appreciation of rhythm should be apparent.

BLOCK 3 — *Improvised class plays to music—teacher's ideas*

From simple group situations the teacher can lead into class situations where either individuals, or small groups, are working towards a common aim. In the early stages the child's awareness of other people will have been limited to his own immediate requirements, but by now he should have mastered his naturally rather self-centred instincts, and be capable of contributing his efforts to group or class activities without undue friction.

Group situations can be joined loosely into class plays, but it is better to limit the dramatic content to interaction between the various groups, rather than giving parts to individuals, and allowing them to carry the plot. For example, three parties of soldiers are attacking a Norman castle with battering rams, etc. Inside the castle are a group of servants. The castle is relieved by the timely arrival of an imaginary company of the king's soldiers, heralded by a distant fanfare of trumpets. The 'Promenade' and the 'Gnome' from Moussorgsky's *Pictures at an Exhibition* provide an excellent stimulus to this class dance drama.

BLOCK 4 — *Improvised class plays to music—children's ideas*

Until now the teacher has provided most of the general ideas, with members of the class contributing such details as they feel able. With practice they should contribute more and more until eventually they provide the whole story, relying on the teacher only to select a potentially exciting piece of music and if necessary link their ideas together.

BLOCK 5 — *Improvised group plays to music—teacher helps groups*

The children will gradually become capable of working and rehearsing in groups on their own, depending on their teacher only to supply the music and sort out the occasional difficulty. For purely practical reasons it is usually necessary for all the groups to work to the same piece of music, although their stories will vary.

BLOCK 6 — *Dance drama*

A natural desire to show some part of the movement work will manifest itself during the third year; with some classes this may come even earlier. This polishing of a movement pattern or story is called dance drama. The children will be eager to ensure that the finished product reaches the highest standard of which they are capable, and will devote considerable time and effort to rehearsal. Although the outward justification, as far as the children are concerned, may be that the work is to be shown, more often than not the real reason is that they enjoy perfecting it for its own sake. The showing of it is still of secondary importance. This desire to perfect and show is the best incentive to movement work among older children. This should be recognised and utilised, but as a means to extending the range of activity rather than as an end in itself. With the help of a few lights and blocks dance drama can be most exciting and highly spectacular. Because of this it is all too easy to concentrate on it as a 'show piece', at the expense of the less spectacular and more important aspects of speech work.

BLOCKS 7-14   Speech

The general aim of all speech work is to increase the potential of the voice as a medium of communication. To do this the child must first gain enough confidence to speak freely. This can only be done by practice. If it is to have the necessary vitality, speech work should be a spontaneous response to realistic situations. When the child has gained confidence, both in the fact that he has something worthwhile to say, and that he is capable of actually saying it, we are in a position to consider clarity and fluency. The former can be dealt with by presenting the child with dramatic situations which require clear speaking; the latter will only come through continual practice at putting thoughts into words. The important thing to remember about all speech work in drama is that it should be the spontaneous result of emotional involvement, and not externally imposed 'speech exercises'.

BLOCK 7 — *Stimulation and control of speech*

The child must first be encouraged to speak freely. This requires confidence. The confidence already acquired through movement can be used by giving the child movement situations which, at some point, require speech, e.g., spectators at a football match cheering a goal. The few children who find real difficulty in spontaneous speech can begin by making their own sounds to accompany their movements, e.g., being animals and making the appropriate noises.

As soon as the child can speak with confidence he must

learn to control his oral responses to his emotions, if he is to express himself accurately. Initially he should only be asked to experiment with the simplest of vocal contrasts, e.g., a conspirator as opposed to a street-corner newsboy. When he can sense the difference between simple isolated situations he can be presented with a more complicated scene requiring contrasts of vocal response, e.g., noisy children in a class-room—enter headmaster.

BLOCK 8 — *Imaginative speech work in pairs and groups —teacher's stimulation*

Having gained experience as an individual within a group, i.e., in crowd work, the child is in a position to control more detailed and specific situations suggested by the teacher. As yet he has had experience only as an isolated individual seeking anonymity within a group, as a cover for any possible self-consciousness. Although he has learned a certain amount of control over his speech, he has not yet learned to control it when in contact with other people. Situations are now presented which demand this oral contact. Work in pairs is the simplest starting-point: for example, an elderly person asks a policeman the way. As experience increases work can be in larger groups.

A glance at Fig. 3, page 128, will show that speech work can now progress along two different lines; one leading quickly to improvisation (block 9); the other concerning itself mainly with speaking as an activity in its own right (blocks 10–14).

BLOCK 9 — *Speech situations in pairs leading to group plays*

Situations in pairs and small groups can now be used as the basis for simple plays: speech situation in pairs—vacuum-cleaner salesman bothering busy housewife; then working in threes and introducing the milkman anxious to have his bill paid; increasing the number to four, the husband arrives home unexpectedly.

This leads naturally into the main-stream (group improvisations) via block 19 on page 54.

BLOCK 10 — *Story-making by teacher from children's ideas*

This work has two main aims. Firstly to give practice in speaking informally, and secondly to help connect ideas. This covers a most important aspect—story-making. Initially the teacher will simply ask the children for ideas. He will then show them how they can be strung together to make a story.

BLOCK 11 — *Story-making by discussion as a class and in groups*

This is the usual forerunner to any lesson involving play-making, and need not be a separate topic, unless practice is obviously needed. By now the responsibility for stringing ideas together rests with the children, e.g., they can be presented with three assorted objects or characters, and asked to make a story round them.

BLOCK 12 — *Stories made up by children on the basis of a given idea*

The children should now be doing most of their own story-making, and will need only the very briefest of suggestions, e.g., the first or last line of a play ("It all began when Johnny got his new bicycle . . ." or ". . . I told you that it was dishonest"). Alternatively an interesting picture or photograph can be used, or an object with potentially strong associations, such as a knife with strange carvings.

The work outlined in blocks 10–12 can be used purely to stimulate speech and imagination, in which case none of the stories need be enacted. Alternatively, stories can be used as a basis for improvised plays (block 19, page 54).

BLOCK 13 — *Speeches, debates, discussions—non-technical speech training*

Somewhere between blocks 11 and 12 more formal speech work can begin. Block 13 covers all forms of speeches, debates and discussions, from a lawyer in a magistrate's court to a debate on nuclear disarmament. The children will find it necessary, particularly where formal speeches are concerned, to have some advice of a simple non-technical nature if their efforts are to be successful: "In order to improve audibility make sure that you address your audience, and don't look at the floor."

BLOCK 14 — *Improvisations based on social situations and problems*

If the teacher has the right relationship with the children, the work in this section will develop quite naturally from points put forward in speeches, debates and discussions. It is an excellent opportunity to help the immature and rather bewildered adolescent to experiment with new adult situations about which he has doubts, e.g., the right way in which to order a meal in a restaurant, or how to answer the telephone correctly. Improvisations of this nature can frequently promote discussion. This should be encouraged.

BLOCKS 15-22   Movement and Speech together —improvised play-making

In this section speech and movement are combined and brought to fruition. All work done on speech and movement, if it is to have life and meaning, should lead to improvisation, and it is through this that the more complicated and realistic situations are tackled. The eventual aim is for the children to learn to work together in small groups, making up and doing their own plays.

These plays may or may not be polished (rehearsed). If they are it will be for one of two reasons. The first and more important is that the children themselves feel the need to reach a worthwhile standard for their own satisfaction. The second will apply only to older children, and will result from a desire to share their creative experiences with their peers. The same happens in the visual arts when the older child is no longer satisfied with painting for its own sake,

D

but needs to display the result and have it appreciated and constructively criticised. This is a natural part of growing up, and should be catered for. The work can still be creative provided the stories are improvised, and a genuine product of the children's ideas. With practice they will learn to offer constructive criticism of each other's plays. Properly handled this is very valuable.

BLOCK 15 — *Movement and speech together—crowd scenes*

This work is closely related to that in block 7 (page 45), where speech was introduced through movement. We now have a crowd scene where the children are moving and speaking together, but still working as individuals, only occasionally making real contact with perhaps close friends in the class; as, for example, on a crowded railway station with everyone absorbed in his particular business, and only occasionally meeting others when he feels he wants to do so. Some may simply be prospective passengers wandering up and down the platform on their own. Others, with more confidence, may choose to be station porters with a word for everyone ("Mind your backs!"). By choosing this type of crowd scene as many children as possible are catered for. In order to encourage those who are reluctant to make any sort of contact it could be suggested that they are all tired holiday-makers trying to find out from which platform their train is leaving.

The action should be kept moving all the time, and as soon as one scene appears to be played out another should be presented. This prevents the children running out of material and becoming embarrassed during the crucial stage, when they are still gaining confidence. Initially much of this work will be crude, and very quickly exhausted, but it can be developed as confidence is gained. The problem will then be to decide when to stop it—the answer is as soon as fresh ideas have run out and the work is becoming repetitious.

BLOCK 16 — *Introduction of incidents into crowd scenes to give simple plots*

When the children can talk and move naturally in crowd scenes they will begin to want something to happen. They will often provide their own suggestions as to what it can be, but the teacher should be careful to choose from them the sort of incidents most likely to affect and bring everyone together, e.g., the train that the holiday-makers are waiting for fails to stop. With practice the situations can be made more complicated, and joined to form simple plots.

Although still working as individuals, the children are now starting to make contact with each other and moving towards a common aim. This is the beginning of the class play.

There are now two possible lines of development. The work can either progress through blocks 18 and 20, in which case it will consist of class and group plays based upon crowd scenes, but made up by the children, or it can progress through blocks 17 and 19, in which case it will consist of class and group plays based upon the teacher's suggestions and hints. This gives the teacher the opportunity of presenting the children with situations he feels will extend them and add to their fund of experiences. Blocks 18 and 20 will be dealt with first.

BLOCK 18 — *Plays made by class discussion from given crowd situations*

The children should now be called upon to devise their own plots, based on crowd scenes presented to them by the teacher. These will usually evolve through discussion with the class after they have experimented with a particular crowd scene. The teacher acts as chairman, making suggestions only when necessary.

In order to get the children used to organising themselves and working in groups, class plays should be evolved which depend upon the interaction of various groups, e.g., a class play based upon a party of explorers arriving at a native village which is expecting to be attacked by bandits. The explorers send back to their base for help (four groups at least). In this kind of situation the individual, although working in a smaller group, is only called upon to ensure that his actions fit in generally with the requirements of the group. He is not yet asked to assume the responsibility for making major decisions likely to affect the general plot.

BLOCK 20 — *Group plays made up by children from given crowd situations*

As soon as the children are used to working together in groups they can be asked to develop situations within their groups. For instance, on seeing the native village, the explorers have to make their own decisions on whether to visit it or not. Likewise the natives have to decide what sort of reception they are going to give the explorers if and when they arrive. One or two children within the group are now called upon to assume the responsibility of reaching decisions.

This is the beginning of the group play arising from crowd situations, e.g., after some crowd work centred on a native village, the class is divided into groups, and each group makes up its own play based on the arrival of the first white man in a native village.

BLOCK 17 — *Improvised class plays based on teacher's suggestions*

In block 16 (page 51) incidents were introduced into the crowd scenes to give some kind of plot or dramatic shape. In block 17 this work is developed to produce the class play. The teacher, by suitable choice of plot, can provide a play in which the action develops through a series of loosely-joined crowd scenes.

It is not necessary to provide naturalistic links from one scene to the next, as children find it quite easy to transfer themselves from, for example, a market-place to a hospital, even though this may necessitate the hurried rearrangement of a few chairs, etc. They will accept this sudden transition as being quite logical, whereas adults, in a similar situation, would probably feel the need for something smoother— a blackout or a curtain between scenes to give time for emotional adjustment. In class plays, however, locations can be unlimited; the first scene may take place in a Chinese market, and the second in a London hospital. Changes of character can be equally drastic, a Chinese coolie easily becoming a house surgeon if the plot demands it. This adaptability gives unlimited scope for story-making.

BLOCK 19 — *Group plays based on teacher's suggestions*

Through their experience of group work within the general structure of class plays, and speech work in pairs and small groups (block 9, page 47), the children should now be able to cope with simple group plays based on suggested stories.

Left to their own devices, however, they will tend to develop extremely complicated but conventional plots, which will frequently be so rambling that the children become confused and lose their absorption. The real trouble here is that although the content of the plot is only too obvious, the method of presentation—the detail—is tortuous and long-winded. It then becomes a process of developing stories through talking about them rather than through *doing* them. Although this in itself is a valuable activity (block 12, page 48), it is not the aim here.

The teacher must, therefore, provide suggestions for plots of a very simple yet evocative nature, where the main plot will stem from the development of the characters involved and the interaction between them, e.g., a simple situation based upon the reactions of a family when a distant relative arrives unexpectedly. Likewise, a story built round a single object, a knife with unusual carvings or a treasure chest, should help to ensure that the story is kept fairly simple.

BLOCK 21 — *Group improvisations*

By now the drama course should have stimulated and developed the children's imaginations, increased their ability to work together, and given them the necessary confidence to express themselves fluently and with some degree of accuracy through their speech and movement. They should now be in a position to plan, develop and organise their own short plays in groups. This is group improvisation. Ideally the teacher should become a sympathetic critic rather than a source of inspiration, providing only an organised atmosphere in which to work. In practice, however, he will usually find that it is necessary to give a helping hand to most of the groups at some time or another.

For this kind of work the class will normally be split into small groups, each one engrossed in its own particular play, and taking little or no notice of the others. The formation of these groups is best left largely to the children themselves. This may sometimes lead to the rejection of the occasional child by all the groups, but if our drama course has been successful, and the teacher is tactful, this problem can be overcome.

Once the groups have prepared their own particular plays, they will usually be keen to show them to the rest of the class. They will be equally keen to see what the other groups have done. This presents a useful opportunity for constructive criticism, by informal discussion after watching the plays, and frequently leads to a valuable exchange of ideas on social and moral problems, e.g., should you in fact refuse to act as a police witness to the accident you saw? At first they may be over-critical about detail in the plays done by other groups, and miss the more important aspects, such as the general structure of the story and the interplay between the characters. With practice, however, critical faculties will develop. The children will begin to understand the making of a good play, and formulate their criticisms accordingly.

BLOCK 22 — *Polished group and class improvisations*

When the children become more critical of their own work, initial attempts will no longer satisfy them, and the opportunity to try again and incorporate suggested improvements will be welcomed. If they find that they cannot achieve the standard they want they will frequently look to the teacher to act as a producer.

They are now beginning to think in terms of 'showing' or theatre, and this is a natural result of growing up. The child still needs and enjoys personal drama, but as he becomes more sophisticated he demands a reason or objective. Theatre is the natural objective; but, as far as the teacher is concerned, it is only a means to an end. Thus, although the teacher will now find himself basing much of the work on presentation for theatre, television or radio, the plays are still initially improvised, and approached through drama.

A play for television based on the story of Christopher Columbus might well be tackled through an interesting movement session on unruly crowds, a storm at sea, sailors loading and working a sailing ship, Red Indians seeing their first white man, and a Spanish dance. After this the class can be divided into groups, each doing a play of its own based on the story of Christopher Columbus.

Alternatively, a combined group improvisation might be attempted in which each group is given the responsibility of organising and producing a particular part of the story. It then rehearses and polishes its own part for presentation. Obviously dance dramas (block 6, page 44) and plays based on social situations and problems (block 14, page 49) can be polished in a similar manner.

Once an attempt is made to polish improvisations it will often be necessary to script at least parts of the work if the play is to follow the agreed pattern. Thus, despite all our earlier remarks on the distinction between adult theatre and child drama, at this point a script can, and often does, have a place in the drama course. Indeed, the teacher may now, if he wishes, use the work as a lead-in to the study of formally scripted plays. This use of child drama as an approach to adult theatre is dealt with more fully in Section 7 (page 135).

4   Practical activities

This section is devoted to answering the ever-present question: "What can I actually do in a drama lesson?" It is impossible to lay out step by step the exact way in which each drama lesson should be tackled. Apart from the varying circumstances, each teacher must approach the work in his own way, and responses will obviously vary from class to class.

It would seem that the best way to help is to list as many examples as possible of activities that can be used to cover each of the steps laid down in Fig. 3, page 128.

Section 5 (page 116) shows how these activities may be drawn upon to plan a drama lesson, and Section 6 (page 124) gives a few general hints on organisation. These suggested activities are only offered as a starting-point from which to develop ideas: in the end every drama teacher must rely on his own inventiveness, often on the spur of the moment.

This section is arranged in the same way as the last one, in that the activities are listed under block headings, although some of them inevitably overlap. Where music is useful, suitable records have been suggested.

BLOCKS 1-6   Movement

RELAXATION

Objective

To rid the body and mind of any previous tensions as an aid to free movement and concentration.

Activities

Relaxation of the body stems from relaxation of the mind. The first requirement is, therefore, to create the kind of atmosphere in which it is possible to relax. This can be done with the help of words and/or music. The following outlines provide possible starting-points.

1. With the children lying on the floor, the teacher describes a relaxing situation, trying to make them as absorbed as possible by the use of vivid description:

    "You are lying on your back in cool grass by the side of a river on a hot day. . . ."

    "You are lying on a lilo floating on the sea, and listening to the gentle lapping of the waves. . . ."

    "You are floating through the air on a magic carpet. Try to sense the effortless floating through space. . . ."

    "You wake up on a clear sunny morning with the bedroom window open. You lie there, completely relaxed, taking deep breaths of the fresh cool air."

    "Imagine that you are a cat lying on a soft hearth-rug in front of a blazing fire."

    "You are relaxing in a bath, enjoying a sense of warmth and well-being."

2. It is just as important to be able to relax when standing, sitting or moving. The following examples will help:

"You are lazily enjoying a shower."

"You are a skin-diver silently and gracefully swimming through the water, enjoying the feeling of weightlessness."

"You are reclining in an easy chair after a heavy and enjoyable meal."

"You are standing on the bridge of a ship, gently moving with the swell."

3. Relaxation will usually be more complete if it is preceded by some form of tension:

"You struggle up the last few feet of a difficult rock face, to collapse tired and triumphant in the heather at the top."

"You lift a heavy box on to a shelf that you can only just reach, and sink back exhausted."

"You are a piece of elastic, stretched out and then let go."

"You are an icicle which slowly melts in the sun—or a candle burning down to a pool of molten wax on the floor."

"You are a puppet being made to dance, when suddenly the strings break."

"You are a Jack-in-a-box held in by the lid, which is suddenly released, whereupon you spring out and remain waving backwards and forwards, eventually coming to a stop."

Music

The atmosphere in some of the more static situations will be helped by the use of suitable music played quietly in the background. This can also be used to extend the period of relaxation after the verbal description has ended. The following pieces of music are useful:

'Berceuse' from *The Firebird*—STRAVINSKY.
'Dawn' and 'Moonlight' from 'Four Sea Interludes' from *Peter Grimes*—BRITTEN.
The Swan of Tuonela—SIBELIUS.
'Adagietto' from *L'Arlésienne* suite—BIZET.

Note: If the children have been relaxed for any length of time they should be brought back to reality gradually to avoid too sudden a change, i.e., play a suitable quiet record which gradually builds up to climax, for example, the end of *The Firebird*.

PURE DANCE

Dance as a medium of expression is, of course, a vast subject in its own right, and no attempt is made here to cover it beyond the limits of a drama course.

Objective

In early movement work, music simply offers a suitable background for specific activities or situations. The next stage is consciously to use the music to suggest the type of movement required at various points in the story. This leads naturally to dance drama, but it should also lead to pure dance—the physical interpretation of a piece of music, in which a story is unnecessary. Music has its own pattern and emotional content, and the aim in pure dance is the physical expression of this pattern and content.

This work has great value in that, if properly handled, it can help children gradually to become conscious of the actual qualities of the music to which they are listening and of the movements which they are making in response to it. When there is a specific activity or story the accompanying music tends to provide only general atmosphere and perhaps one or two 'cues'. 'Pure' movement to the melody, rhythm, polyphony or to the total kinaesthetic impact of a piece of music, demands careful listening and judicious movement. This is of value both to the understanding of music and to the movement, *provided an analytical approach is avoided*.

In drama one does not want to have the children building self-conscious compositions with pieces of movement (light, heavy, etc.) which they have learnt how to 'do'. This part of the work, above all others, needs to remain intuitive.

Activities

The following suggestions are offered as a starting-point.

1. To a drum beat establish three well-contrasted postures (e.g., (a) high and narrow, (b) wide and low, (c) anything different from (a) and (b)). Now link them together by moving from (a) to (b) to (c), in slow motion to slow music.

   Now change the music to fast and light, fast and strong, etc.

2. (a) Make a statue group of 'sport'.
   (b) Make a statue group of 'farming'.
   (c) Change from (a) to (b) on a drum beat.
   (d) Change from (a) to (b) in six sharp, drum-beat steps.
   (e) Change from (a) to (b) to a long musical phrase.
3. In pairs make patterns with your right hands—up, down, side to side, round and round, over, under, quick, slow, backwards and forwards, etc., etc. Now begin, in your pattern-making, to take something from, or fit yourselves to, this music.

Music

Initially, children will enjoy learning to respond quickly, and the music chosen should encourage fairly free movement with sudden energetic responses—jumps, leaps or falls—recurring intermittently. Later the music can become more sophisticated. The main problem is to find suitable musical extracts—below are a few that have been found successful:

The Thunder and Lightning Polka
   (use the section about a third of the way through, with the syncopated crashes)
Les Patineurs—MEYERBEER
   (particularly 'Entrée' and 'Pas de Seul')
Rodeo—COPLAND
   (particularly the quieter parts of 'Buckaroo Holiday')
Billy the Kid—COPLAND
   ('The Gunfight')
Job—VAUGHAN WILLIAMS
   ('The Dance of Job's Comforters')
Swedish Rhapsody— RAY MARTIN

Carnival of the Animals—SAINT-SAËNS
  ('Elephants' and 'Fossils')
Háry János—KODALY
  ('Battle and Defeat of Napoleon')
Divertissement—IBERT
  ('Finale')
Le Bourgeois Gentilhomme—RICHARD STRAUSS
  ('The Banquet')
Tam o' Shanter—MALCOLM ARNOLD
  (the opening)
Sabre Dance—KHACHATURIAN

USE OF POETRY IN MOVEMENT

In the same way that a child will respond to the stimulus of
percussion or music, he will respond to the sound of the
human voice. The way in which he responds will depend
not only upon the sense of the words, but also upon the
inflections, volume and pitch of the voice. Even if the words
are unintelligible the child will respond to the voice as a
sound. It follows, therefore, that the teacher is not limited to
using his voice only to convey intelligible meaning; he can
also rely purely on the sounds he makes to stimulate movement. Lines such as:

  ". . . sent spinning, dipping, slipping, shuffled by a heavy-
    handed wind,
  shifted sideways, sifted, lifted, and in swarms made to fly
  spent sun-flies, gorgeous tatters, airdrift, pinions of trees,"

will stimulate movement because they have an intelligible
meaning as well as the right sounds. But the first verse of

Jabberwocky, appropriately spoken, will also stimulate movement, even though the words themselves have no immediately apparent meaning.

> "'Twas brillig, and the slithy toves
> Did gyre and gimble in the wabe.
> All mimsy were the borogoves,
> And the mome raths outgrabe."

The whole of *Jabberwocky* could be used to stimulate a class movement play. Everyone could experiment with the movements described in the first and last verses. A group of children could become the Jabberwocky, and the remainder of the class could become either mothers or boys, and act appropriately while the poem is being spoken.

There are great possibilities in this field, not only through the child moving to someone else's narration, but also to his own, as for example, when he sinks (reciting)

> "Down, down, down,
> Down to the depths of the sea,"

or, finding himself alone, goes

> ". . . tiptoe to the telephone
> And summons the immediate aid
> Of London's noble Fire Brigade!"

From moving to the onomatopoeia, as well as the prose meaning of the words, the speaking tends to come alive with a spontaneity which children seldom acquire from the formal study of poetry. Conversely, an exhilarating movement experience can be made to feed the urge for rhythmic language, and so lead children on to speak or write poems

E

of their own. Again, the imaginative teacher will readily see the possibility of taking a theme like 'Fear' or 'Town and Country', and developing it with a class in terms of movement, music and poetry-speaking, with some of the poems culled from anthologies and others created by the children. Working, as it does, upon the springs of experience, drama again and again exposes the artificiality of subject frontiers.

BLOCK I — *Stimulation and control of movement*

STIMULATION OF MOVEMENT

Objective

To encourage free movement. The problem here is to break down the initial barrier of self-consciousness. Ways of overcoming this are:

To ensure that all the children are working at the same time.

To ensure that the activities are enjoyable and within the children's experience.

To use activities involving vigorous action, such as sword fighting.

To push the lessons along at such a rate that the children never really have time to become self-conscious, but, at the same time, being careful not to sacrifice sincerity and absorption for speed.

To use sound or music to create a suitable atmosphere, to stimulate movement and to relax tension generally.

Activities

1. Bouncing imaginary tennis balls in as many different ways as possible—quickly, slowly, behind the back, on one leg, high, low, etc. (*Little Rock Getaway*—LES PAUL.)
2. Dancing marionettes. (*Whistlin' Rufus*—CHRIS BARBER; *Jazz Pizzicato*—LEROY ANDERSON; early RUSS CONWAY records.)
3. Snowball fights.
4. Delivering newspapers. (*Messenger Boy*—RON GOODWIN.)
5. Comic billposters. (*Jumpin' Bean*—SIDNEY TORCH.)
6. Swordfighting. (*Romeo and Juliet*—TCHAIKOWSKI.)
7. Playing a musical instrument to any suitably lively music.
8. A storm at sea on a tea clipper. ('Storm' from *Peter Grimes*—BENJAMIN BRITTEN.)
9. Being attacked by a swarm of wasps. (*The Flight of the Bumble Bee*—RIMSKY KORSAKOV.)

CONTROL OF MOVEMENT

Objective

The adjustment and control of their movements to suit various situations. This work is best approached initially through the use of sound, aiming first only at simple distinctions.

Activities

1. A game of 'statues'—everybody moving while the record is playing, and freezing into statues whenever it stops.

2. Walking round to a drum beat; following its variations; stopping whenever the drum beat stops; changing direction sharply on every loud beat, etc.

3. Playing tennis at normal speed (*Little Rock Getaway*), changing to slow motion when the music changes (*Narcissus*).

4. Puppets in boxes, lifted by tugs at strings (drum beat); made to dance (record); collapsing to floor when strings break (record stops). (*Whistlin' Rufus* by CHRIS BARBER or *Roulette* by RUSS CONWAY.)

5. Playing with a heavy medicine ball (*Narcissus*), and then as a contrast with a light beach ball (*Little Rock Getaway*).

6. Working a machine with hands and feet. (*Syncopated Clock*—LEROY ANDERSON; 'March' from *The Love of Three Oranges*—PROKOFIEV.)

7. Pursuing a wary butterfly, mouse or rabbit.

8. Burglars creeping through a stately home in the dark, and being surprised by occasional noises (drum beats); exploring a cave; finding the way through a mine-field or walking on thin ice. (Opening of first movement from *Concerto for Orchestra*—BARTÔK; parts from 'Mars' —HOLST.)

9. Underwater diving, first in a heavy diving suit, then in the comparative freedom of a frogman's outfit. (*Swan of Tuonela*—SIBELIUS; 'Dawn' from *Peter Grimes*—BENJAMIN BRITTEN.)

10. Exploring a planet where there is very little gravity ('Aquarium' from *The Carnival of Animals*—SAINT-SAËNS).

11. Dusting weird objects in a museum with a feather duster ('Pizzicato' from *Sylvia*—DELIBES).

❋ 12. Writing one's name on the ceiling with a long-handled paint-brush, or in the sand with one's big toe.

13. Imagining that the floor is a beach, and making patterns in the sand with bare feet, covering as much ground as possible (any lively record).

14. Conducting an orchestra (any record which includes obvious contrasts).

15. Selecting three different statues, and changing quickly from one to another on a drum beat; then changing slowly to a sustained sound (cymbal hit with felt striker).

BLOCK 2 — *Imaginative movement, individually and in pairs and groups—teacher's stimulation*

Objective

To give the child the opportunity of dealing with emotional situations requiring more complex movement. This will not only enlarge his emotional experience, but will also develop confidence in his ability to express himself through movement. Situations should be chosen which it is natural to interpret through movement rather than speech, but the teacher should not actively discourage any spontaneous speech that may arise. The main problem here is to stimulate the child's imagination so that he can:

1. Comprehend and believe in the situation sufficiently to become inwardly absorbed in it.

2. Sustain this absorption long enough to make the experience worthwhile.

3. Appreciate the situation sufficiently to give the point or climax the necessary build-up.

In order to do this the teacher must choose his situations carefully. They should be clear-cut and brief, with obvious conflicts leading up to strong climaxes.

Activities

1. You are carrying a large box of glasses through a crowded department store, when suddenly you are attacked by a persistent wasp. Eventually either the box is dropped, the wasp is swatted, or both. (Walking through store—*Messenger Boy* by RON GOODWIN; wasp—*Flight of the Bumble Bee*—RIMSKY KORSAKOV.)

2. Chase and eventually catch a mouse that has escaped into an old attic full of junk. ('Pizzicato' from *Sylvia*—DELIBES.)

3. Take a book from the pocket of a sleeping friend.

4. Take the key to your handcuffs from the belt of a dozing guard, and escape before he wakes up.

5. A photographer posing his model and taking a picture. Photographers arrange models, and on the start of a 'count down' by the teacher the model prepares to freeze while the photographer prepares to take the picture, which is done on a hand-clap or drum beat after the 'count down'.

6. Carefully feel your way across a minefield, and rescue an injured friend who has to be brought back to safety. (Sound effects of distant explosions and machine-gun fire.)

7. You are a scientist controlling a robot from a portable panel connected to the robot by wires. ('March' from *The Love of Three Oranges*—PROKOFIEV.)

8. Sword fights in pairs, movement varying according to

the type of sword used. As no actual physical contact is necessary this is a good way of giving the children the opportunity to fight without everyone ending up in a heap on the floor (control). (Either 'The Storm' from *Peter Grimes*—BENJAMIN BRITTEN, as general 'fight' noise, or the end of *Romeo and Juliet*—TCHAIKOVSKY, as a more controlled exercise with a definite climax.)

9. Rescuing a fellow explorer from a dangerous tropical swamp. ('Samuel Goldenberg and Schmuyle' from *Pictures at an Exhibition*—MOUSSORGSKY.)

10. Circus: jugglers, clowns, animal trainers, strong men, tightrope walkers, etc. (*Entry of the Gladiators*, 'The Polka' from *Façade*, *Orpheus in the Underworld* and *Carnival of the Animals*.)

11. Rescuing belongings from a fire, leading up to a climax either of the fire being extinguished or of the building collapsing. ('Sacrifice' from *The Rite of Spring*—STRAVINSKY.)

12. Storm at sea and a shipwreck. ('Storm' from *Peter Grimes*.)

13. Climbers in a blizzard in the Alps being buried by an avalanche. (*Night on a Bare Mountain*—MOUSSORGSKY.)

14. Washing and grooming an elephant. ('Finale' from *Divertissement*—IBERT.)

15. Lords and ladies dressing for a coronation. This can be done in pairs, one child acting as the reflection of the other in a mirror. ('Pizzicato' from *Sylvia*—DELIBES.)

16. Removal men trying to manœuvre a grand piano through a narrow doorway, and along a narrow passage.

17. Gangs of sailors working a sailing ship, and singing a sea-shanty as they work.

18. A situation based on a group of people passing buckets of water from hand to hand in an effort to put out a fire. (Last section of *The Sorcerer's Apprentice*—DUKAS.)

19. A band of street musicians assemble and begin to play their instruments. Suddenly an irate householder, no longer able to contain his fury, hurls a bucket of water at the musicians from an upstairs window. They flee in disorder.

20. A pit stop during a Grand Prix motor race, the emphasis being on speed and efficiency.

BLOCK 3 — *Improvised class plays to music—teacher's ideas*

Objective

To give the children the opportunity of contributing their individual or small group efforts towards a class activity. The main problem here is to keep everybody occupied. This can be done by ensuring that the story depends not on individual performances, but on the interaction between various groups. This necessitates broad, simple plots outlined by such obvious cues as the banging of a drum, the crash of cymbals or the ringing of a bell. A more complex sound cue could be the entry of a court procession on hearing the *Trumpet Voluntary*.

In this way, the teacher is able to control the action, moving the story along by the use of his cues when he feels that the children are ready. Alternatively, the whole play may be based on a longer piece of music which contains the changes of mood required.

Activities

1. Three groups: villagers in local hostelry; villagers at home; Martians.

   People in 'pub' hear strange whining noise, all go outside to see what it is, and are just in time to see a strange luminous sphere descend into a nearby wood. As quietly as possible, they go and persuade their friends and neighbours to leave their television sets, gathering any weapons they can find. The whole party then apprehensively approaches the wood from which a fierce glow is emanating. They climb the low wall that borders the wood, and fan out as they begin to creep through the undergrowth. (Fade in the second half of 'Mars' from *The Planets*—HOLST, beginning with the quiet, 'creepy' part.) As the climax of the music approaches, the villagers reach the sphere and try to get near to it, but are driven back by the intense heat. As they stand watching, on the first crash of the musical climax the top of the sphere seems to vanish, and strange robot-like figures emerge. The remainder of the action can be worked out round the devastation wrought upon the village and the villagers by the Martians.

2. Three groups: villagers, priests and explorers.

   Explorers hacking their way through the Malayan jungle. Natives in a nearby village are going about their normal business, with the exception of a few, who are passing on local news by drum beat. This drum beat provides a rhythm for both groups. On the crash of a cymbal, the explorers suddenly see an ornate temple in a clearing. Unknown to the explorers this cymbal crash is a warning to the local villagers that their temple has been discovered.

The drum beat stops. The villagers gather their weapons and silently hurry towards the temple. Meanwhile, a second cymbal crash has heralded the appearance, on the temple steps, of a number of priests. For a moment, the priests and explorers stare at each other. The explorers then seem to decide what to do and, without a word, push the priests aside and enter the temple intent upon stealing its treasures. To a slow and menacing drum beat, the armed villagers begin to encircle the temple. The drum continues while the explorers are helping themselves. Having taken as much of the treasure as they can carry, they decide to leave. As they appear on the steps the drum beat stops and the explorers find themselves facing a silent and menacing circle of natives. On the crash of another cymbal, the priests move forward to reclaim the treasure, and the natives raise their spears. The explorers, realising that the game is up, hand back the treasure. The slow drum beat starts again and is the signal for the natives to fall back, leaving a narrow lane of escape for the explorers. The latter move off, gradually gathering speed as the tempo of the drum beat increases. It quickly builds to a climax of a final cymbal crash, which is the sign for all the villagers to raise a great shout of triumph. They turn to offer their thanksgivings to the priests. The crash has arrested the explorers' flight, and they stop, turn, and watch this unusual ceremony.

3. Coronation scene. Including royal procession, arrival of unexpected guests and actual crowning sequence as a conclusion.

4. Earthmen arriving on new planet. Their spaceship arrives, they alight and, after accustoming themselves to

the lack of gravity, begin to explore. They meet the inhabitants of the planet and are taken to their ruler, where they exchange gifts, are entertained and eventually return to the spaceship. Alternatively, the reception could be hostile.

5. Battle scene. Opposing armies fight (using imaginary swords). After the battle, relatives from both sides appear looking for their dead and wounded kin. Looters might be seen at the same time, looking for booty.

6. Fire of London. Begins with Londoners trying to extinguish fire and salvage what is left of their possessions ('Dance of King Kastchei' from *The Firebird*). They are unsuccessful, and lose almost everything. There is a general air of despondency. Eventually they decide to rebuild (the last few minutes of Bartók's *Concerto for Orchestra*). Having rebuilt, they celebrate with a dance (any gay polka).

7. A ritual sacrifice. Children bring any small improvised percussion instrument they can think of. Do some preliminary work on adding these sounds to a basic beat provided by a leader, to give a strong rhythm for the ritual dance. Place a low block in the centre of the hall floor as a focal point or altar. The story begins with the leader awakening the villagers with his slow even drum beat. Gradually the villagers add their own sounds as they gather round the altar. Some begin to dance to the rhythm, others are content to remain seated. The sound and the dance increase in pace as the climax draws near, until with a final crash everyone stops. A cymbal crashes, and the high priest appears. He mounts the rostrum, looks round slowly, and eventually points out the

unfortunate victim, who is seized and placed upon the altar at the high priest's feet. The onlookers begin a low chant, which increases in speed and pitch as they raise their (imaginary) knives. As it reaches its climax, the villagers sink their knives into the body of the victim with a shout of triumph. This is followed by absolute silence.

8. The museum. Everyone becomes a museum exhibit (animal or human). Choose one of the human exhibits to be a future 'centre of interest'. (There will often be a statue resembling someone like Nelson or Napoleon.) This character should occupy a prominent position. At the stroke of midnight (cymbals) all the exhibits come to life. Fade-in music ('The Battle and Defeat of Napoleon' from *Háry János*—KODALY). Use the early part of the music to explore the museum. Intuitively the exhibits sense that the main character is hostile, and they begin, very slowly, to use some sort of witchcraft on him— strange magical signs cast over him from afar. As the music gathers towards a climax, they press closer and closer towards him, until eventually he has no alternative but to return to his pedestal. (This should be timed to fit the climax.) In the quiet passage that follows, the other exhibits seem content to return slowly to their places and become inanimate once more.

9. Symbolic group expression of war and peace. Divide the class into four groups. Give all the groups time to work out corporate statues expressing war, peace, refugees, and opulent, ostentatious victors. Allocate each group a corner of the hall. On a given signal (drum beat) the groups must be ready to become these statues. Pair off war with peace, and refugees with victors. On a given music

cue the statues dismantle themselves, and war approaches peace, refugees approach victors, maintaining the emotion and attitude of the statue. Without touching, the two groups intermingle, and pass by each other, as the climax of sound is reached. The sound recedes and we discover that as they passed, each group exchanged identity. Peace now represents war, and is heading in a warlike fashion towards the appropriate position where it will become a statue representing war. Refugees and victors will have effected a similar exchange. Likewise, the statues now representing war can be exchanged with refugees, and peace with opulent victors. This activity requires considerable concentration on the part of the children if it is to succeed, and the movement needs to be slow and controlled to ensure a gradual transition. There should be no speech. The movement should be controlled by the sound stimulus which can be either cymbals used to create a climax at the point of transition, followed by a long anti-climax, or a suitable piece of music (the end of the 'Berceuse' and 'Finale' of *The Firebird*).

BLOCK 4 — *Improvised class plays to music—children's ideas*

Objective

To encourage the children to think and decide for themselves the emotions evoked by a particular piece of music, so that a story can be evolved from these ideas. The main problem here is that so many diverse ideas will be forthcoming that the children will generally be unable to contrive a story to include them all. The teacher will usually find that he has to select the most promising ideas and help the children work out a story from them.

Music

Obviously the only suggestions that can be included here are those for suitable music, likely to produce ideas for a story from the children.

Night on the Bare Mountain—MOUSSORGSKY.
Romeo and Juliet—TCHAIKOVSKY.
'Hall of the Mountain King' from *Peer Gynt*—GRIEG.
'The Dance of Job's Comforters' from *Job*—VAUGHAN WILLIAMS.
Billy the Kid—COPLAND.
Rodeo—COPLAND.
Fanfare for the Common Man—COPLAND.
Peter Grimes—BENJAMIN BRITTEN ('Four Sea Interludes' and 'Passacaglia').
Pictures at an Exhibition—MOUSSORGSKY.
'Satan's Dance of Triumph' from *Job*—VAUGHAN WILLIAMS.

BLOCK 5 — *Improvised group plays to music—teacher helps groups*

Objective

To give the children the opportunity to work out their own movement ideas in greater detail, and to make up stories from these ideas. By this time the children should be working well in groups, and be capable of sorting out ideas and rehearsing on their own. For practical reasons all groups will have to make up their stories to the same piece of music. The teacher should ensure that the extract or piece of music is reasonably short, and that it does not contain passages which strain the concentration too much, e.g., a long quiet passage requiring prolonged grief. Likewise, the music should have fairly definite climaxes and changes of mood upon which to base a story.

Music

Some suitable music has already been mentioned in previous sections, but the following list should provide a solid basis from which to start. If the teacher is prepared to edit the music he will widen the scope considerably.

'Mars' from *The Planets*—HOLST (second half).
Ritual Fire Dance—DE FALLA.
The Sorcerer's Apprentice—DUKAS (edited).
Danse Macabre—SAINT-SAËNS (edited).
'The Market Place at Limoges' leading to 'The Catacombs' from *Pictures at an Exhibition*—MOUSSORGSKY.
'Berceuse' and 'Finale' from *The Firebird*—STRAVINSKY.
Slaughter on Tenth Avenue—ROGERS and HART.
'Passacaglia' from *Peter Grimes*—BENJAMIN BRITTEN.

BLOCK 6 — *Dance Drama*

A dance drama may be based upon a story to music, or may simply be a movement pattern to music. A football game to the 'Popular Song' from *Façade* may include no more story than perhaps a goal scored on the last note. Interest would come from the diversity and timing of the movement. Even if there is a story, it need not be strictly naturalistic. Occasionally it is worth trying work based upon such obvious abstractions as gluttony, greed, good or evil. 'The Dance of Job's Comforters' may provide a basis for work of this type.

Music

In choosing music for polished dance drama work, twentieth-century composers are usually the best source. The problem is for the teacher to find time to listen to a wide enough variety of music. There is, for example, tremendous scope in Bartôk's *Concerto for Orchestra*, but careful listening is needed to find the most usable parts. The teacher should not be afraid to join together two or three extracts from different records. Try using the quieter part of 'Mars' followed immediately by 'The Infernal Dance of King Kastchei' from *The Firebird*. Some *musique concrète* is suitable, but only use parts that are reasonably predictable. Modern jazz or 'pop' music occasionally produces a useful record. At the time of writing Sandy Nelson's Hit Parade disc *Let There be Drums* has been used for an exciting rhythmic street fight. Leonard Bernstein's music for *West Side Story* (which has been recorded as a ballet suite without words) provides a wealth of useful material.

All the following records contain possibilities for the teacher who is prepared to spend time listening to them, and deciding how to use them. For dramatic work of any type some recordings will be found more suitable than others, and in the Appendix some particularly suitable recordings have been recommended.

LEROY ANDERSON   *The Typewriter.*
ARNOLD   *Tam o' Shanter.*

BARTÔK	*Concerto for Orchestra.*
	The Miraculous Mandarin.
	Music for Strings, Percussion and Celesta.
BERNSTEIN	Ballet music for *West Side Story.*
CARLOS CHAVEZ	*Toccata for Percussion.*
COPLAND	*Rodeo.*
	Billy the Kid.
	El Salon Mexico.
	Appalachian Spring.
	Fanfare for the Common Man.
GERSHWIN	*An American in Paris.*
HOLST	*The Planets.*
IBERT	*Divertissement for Chamber Orchestra.*
	Dance of the Clowns.
KODALY	*Háry János.*
LECOCQ	*La Fille de Madame Angot.*
SANDY NELSON	*Let There be Drums.*
MILHAUD	*Concerto for Percussion and small Orchestra.*
	La Création du Monde.
	La Bœuf sur la Tête.
MOUSSORGSKY	*Pictures at an Exhibition.*
PROKOFIEV	*The Love of Three Oranges.*
	Lt. Kije.
RAVEL	*Mother Goose suite.*
DAVID ROSE	*The Stripper.*
STRAVINSKY	*The Rite of Spring.*
	The Firebird suite.
VAUGHAN WILLIAMS	*Job.*
	The Wasps.
WALTON	*Façade.*

F

BLOCKS 7-14   Speech

BLOCK 7 — *Stimulation and control of speech*

STIMULATION

Objective

1. To put the children into situations which encourage a flow of speech.
2. To give the speech vitality by making it emerge as part of a rhythmic bodily activity.

Activities

1. Felling a tree to drum beats leading up to a climax. As the tree falls there is a loud shout of "Timber!"
2. Prehistoric men trying to communicate with each other by means of gestures and grunts.
3. Cranking a car which eventually splutters into life. The children make their own sound effects.
4. A weight-lifter making appropriate noises as he attempts to lift the weights.
5. Walking round the hall in time to a varying drum beat without touching anybody, but saying "Excuse me", whenever there is a collision.
6. Trying to coax a reluctant cat down from a tree.
7. Training a dog, horse, elephant or flea.
8. A newsboy selling papers.
9. A town-crier with an important message for the people.
10. Directing a car into a tight parking space.
11. Working a machine and making the noises of the machine as it starts, works slowly to top speed, and then runs down to stillness.

CONTROL

Objective

To encourage adjustment and control of speech to suit various situations. The teacher should ensure that all the children are working at the same time, and that they are asked, at this stage, to respond only to simple contrasts.

Activities

1. A solemn coronation scene ending with three lusty cheers as the king is crowned.
2. Section of a football crowd. One person (perhaps the teacher) acts as the referee with a whistle—the crowd responds.
3. An excited party of tourists enter a cathedral, reacting to the change of atmosphere as t ey do so. Use an organ music cue to indicate the change.
4. A crowd awaiting the appearance of the Queen, and responding to her entry.
5. Soldiers creeping up on the enemy and attacking with loud shouts on a given signal.
6. Alone in your bedroom, gradually boiling up inside over a personal injustice, you lose your temper, shout out in anger and accidentally break something you value very much—a model ship or a favourite ornament. Your anger is forgotten as you try to repair the damage.
7. Noisy choirboys preparing for the service, and then quietly and sedately entering the church.
8. A crowd of peasants greet the appearance of a cartload of French aristocrats on their way to the guillotine.

9. A group of holiday-makers suddenly see an unsuspecting oarsman heading for a dangerous weir.
10. A crowd gathers at a house where an ambulance has drawn up.
11. A crowd watching anxiously as a fireman struggles to rescue a small child from a tenth-storey window-ledge.
12. A group of people gather casually round a hole in the road.
13. An angry crowd outside a theatre demanding its money back after the non-appearance of a pop singer.

BLOCK 8 — *Imaginative speech work in pairs and groups —teacher's stimulation*

Objective

To present the children with situations which encourage them to extend and develop their range of oral contact.

Activities (in pairs)

1. Directing a stranger.
2. A door-to-door salesman attempting to sell a vacuum cleaner to a busy housewife.
3. An estate agent showing a prospective house purchaser over a house.
4. A passenger who has lost his ticket trying to explain the fact to a suspicious ticket collector.
5. Trying to borrow money from a friend.
6. Visiting a sick relative in hospital.
7. Trying to explain to an important visitor how a complicated piece of machinery works.
8. A farmer discovers a small boy up a tree stealing apples.

9. Breaking the news as tactfully as possible to a close friend (or a complete stranger) that his wife, mother or son has met with an accident.
10. Making a statement to a policeman after witnessing an accident.
11. Answering a knock at the door to find a scruffy looking tramp begging for money, clothing or a meal.
12. Collecting money for a good cause.
13. Photographer arranging his model and taking various pictures.

Should the first attempts at the above examples tend to lack vitality, the situations should be modified to encourage the type of response required, e.g., directing a stranger may produce good language flow but lack audibility, so modify the situation to directing a slightly deaf old woman. Likewise, making a statement to a policeman about an accident might find both parties stuck for words, so make the situation more specific, i.e., a suspicious policeman on duty at six in the morning stops a stranger who is hurrying down the high street dragging a dustbin. . . .

Activities (in groups)

1. A small party of tourists being conducted round a museum, art gallery, stately home or theatre.
2. A youth club committee meeting.
3. A hairdresser's shop.
4. A group of workers discussing whether to strike or not.
5. A family reunion.
6. A crowd round a stall in a market.
7. A group of sailors working a ship, shouting to each other above a storm.

8. A party of happy holiday-makers on their way to Blackpool.

9. A group of people watching a washing-machine demonstration.

10. Watching television. A member of a family comes home with an exciting piece of news but finds the other members watching their favourite TV programme.

All these situations can quite easily be developed into simple group plays by introducing an unusual incident, and quite naturally lead into block 9. There is also a progression through blocks 10-14, where the main emphasis is upon speaking as an activity in its own right.

BLOCK 9 — *Speech situations in pairs, leading to group plays*

Objective

To build up group plays from simple speech situations by adding characters and incidents. This is one of the methods of approaching group improvisations (see block 20, page 103).

Activities

1. *situation:* An old lady loses her glasses down a drain— a passer-by comes to her aid.
   development: Add to this a helpful policeman, his suspicious inspector, a drain cleaner and a valuable necklace.

2. *situation:* Two elderly women in a train compartment returning from a holiday.

development: A suspicious-looking character enters the compartment with a small suitcase, apparently ticking. The communication cord is pulled and the guard demands an explanation.

3. *situation:* A family having tea.
   development: The radio is switched on for the football results. Growing excitement as the results are announced. Was the coupon posted?

4. *situation:* Buying a pair of shoes.
   development: A lost purse—another customer acts suspiciously—an argument. The manager is called.

5. *situation:* A family returning from a holiday abroad is going through the customs.
   development: A mysterious parcel is discovered in one of the children's suitcases.

6. *situation:* A railway carriage full of assorted passengers.
   development: The train suddenly stops in a dark tunnel. The carriage begins to fill with steam.

7. *situation:* Workers in a factory.
   development: Somebody gets a hand trapped in a machine.

8. *situation:* A party of hikers stop for a picnic.
   development: Add an interesting discovery and a bull.

9. *situation:* A motorist and his passenger discover that they have a puncture but no jack.
   development: A policeman appears and informs them that they are in a 'No Waiting' area.

10. *situation:* A party of cannibals captures an indignant local missionary.

development: Add a large cooking pot and a fire. Suddenly an American frozen foods' representative appears, followed by bearers carrying well-stocked portable refrigerators.

11. *situation:* Vacuum-cleaner salesman attempting to sell cleaner to housewife on washing day.

    development: Add to this the milkman wanting his bill paid, an unexpected visitor, and the husband returning home early.

12. *situation:* An estate agent showing a prospective purchaser over a house.

    development: Add to this an unusual discovery, an argument and the arrival of the owner of the house with a plumber.

BLOCKS 10 – 12 — *Story-making*

Mention has already been made in Section 3, page 47, of the kind of work involved in these blocks. As this is mainly concerned with story-making by the children it is impossible to do more here than suggest a few starting-points.

Although, for the sake of convenience, the following ideas are divided into three sections, it will often be found useful to combine them, e.g., a story might be based on a left luggage office (3.), an African spear (1.), and the opening sentence, "Why didn't you telephone the police?" (2.). It may also be found useful to add one or two characters, particularly in the early stages of the work.

Suggested objects round which a story may be built:

A number of everyday objects may be used (either

singly or in twos and threes), and a story built up round them. However, the children's imaginations will often be better stimulated if an unusual object is included. Again, if the objects selected are easily available for the children to handle and use, it will help.

A stone with strange colouring.
An item of valuable or unusual jewellery.
A pair of spectacles.
A false moustache.
A mask.
An unusual box or casket.
A Roman soldier's helmet.
An African spear.
A skull.
An old coin.
A telegram.
An old map.

2. Suggested first or last lines on which a story may be based:

"I still say we should have gone the other way."
"But she promised that she wouldn't say anything."
"Something must have gone wrong. It's five o'clock already."
"Why didn't you telephone the police?"
"Would you like to try one of these instead, madam?"
"But I said they were too short, not too long!"
"It doesn't matter what we say, no-one will ever believe us."
"We'll all end up in prison for this."

"This is an emergency. Can you tell me where the nearest fish and chip shop is?"

"You can laugh, but what's my mum going to say when she sees that it's green not brown?"

"Switch it off, quick! Look, there are sparks coming out of his ears!!"

3. Suggested locations round which a story may be built:

The inside of a space ship about to land on the moon.
A hole in a wall.
A bombed house.
A scrap-merchant's yard.
A dentist's waiting room.
A police station.
A left-luggage office.
The inside of a large refrigerator.
Inside a lift.
Speaker's Corner in Hyde Park.
Inside a pyramid.
A bank vault.
In a ship's hold with a time bomb.
A youth club.
A secret tunnel.
An attic.
An old theatre.

BLOCK 13 — *Speeches, debates, discussions—non-technical speech training*

The aim here is to apply the confidence and fluency, which the children have gained through drama, to teaching them to express themselves in more formal situations.

Discussion on topics of general interest is usually the easiest starting-point. When experience has been gained the more formal debate can be introduced, and finally the extremely difficult art of 'public speaking' can be attempted.

The most natural approach to discussions and debates is through practical work done in drama. Children are placed in situations in which they have perforce to learn how to discuss.

For example, if they have been doing group plays based on some form of racial tolerance the next drama lesson might well be devoted to a general debate on the subject. Drama lays as much store by the discussion of the plays as by the plays themselves. Indeed, most drama lessons, particularly in the later stages (block 14, page 92), should provide considerable opportunity for this type of work.

At first it is quite probable that the teacher will find himself making most of the running, especially if the children have only a limited background of drama, but once they have gained some confidence, much interesting and valuable work will result, particularly if the teacher is prepared to make use of topical and controversial subjects.

The children gain from their improvisation not only confidence and flow, but awareness of the fact that there are many different kinds of speech appropriate to varying characters and situations (see block 9, page 86). This awareness, and the practical need to master differing kinds of speech, prepare the way for exercises in breathing, diction and the sound of English.

BLOCK 14 — *Improvisations based on social situations and problems*

Objective

Either to promote discussion on a social problem by basing an improvisation on it, or to clarify ideas already discussed by basing an improvisation on them.

Activities

The following social problems are suggested as possible starting-points:

1. Situations based upon the relationships between adolescents and their parents.

   The thoughtless teenager arrives home two hours later than expected.

   Father tackles a teenager about spending too much money on pop records.

   Mother has an argument with her teenage daughter who refuses to help at home.

   A teenager brings home a friend whom his (her) parents feel is a bad influence on him (her).

2. Situations based on teenagers' attitudes towards the law.

   A teenager who has witnessed an accident refuses to make a statement—he doesn't want to help the police.

   A policeman discovers a group of teenagers breaking the windows of a cricket pavilion late at night.

   In the cinema one evening a teenager witnesses a group of acquaintances ripping seats. He is later questioned by the manager and a policeman. What happens?

A teenager discovers that his sister's boy friend is a policeman. What happens?

A call at the local police station to report the loss of your purse or wallet.

A policeman calls on a routine enquiry: "Where were you at a certain time, and do you remember seeing anything of the object of the enquiry?"

3. Situations based on teenagers' attitudes towards each other.

Teenagers make fun of one of their fellows because he is dressed differently from them. An argument follows.

Teenagers discuss why one of their fellows has accepted an apprenticeship in preference to the easy money they are earning as unskilled workers.

Teenagers plan to beat up a coloured boy who is going out with one of their sisters. One lad objects, and an argument ensues.

The committee of a youth club discusses what to do with one of the members who has deliberately broken a piece of club property.

You are about to leave to 'baby-sit' for a relative when a crowd of friends arrives and tries to persuade you to go to a dance with them.

A youth discovers that his girl friend has been invited to a party without him on the night usually reserved for a visit to the cinema. What happens?

4. Situations based on teenagers' attitudes towards employers.

Workmates try to persuade an apprentice to take part

in an unofficial strike. He considers their reasons frivolous. What happens?

An employer is asked for a day off or a rise in pay.

An employer finds out that a clerk has been making private telephone calls from the office. The clerk is called in to see him. (The teacher points out the fallacy in the argument "Everyone else does it—why shouldn't I?")

An office boy has made arrangements to go to a dance in the evening. His employer asks him to remain behind to finish an urgent job. What happens?

A school-leaver has just been called for an interview for a job he particularly wants. He tries to sell himself to his prospective employer.

5. Situations based on teenagers and society generally.

A knock at the door reveals a fellow teenager collecting for famine relief. What happens?

A teenager tries to persuade some friends to form a group to make regular visits to local old-age pensioners.

A group of teenagers is illegally skylarking about in a shop doorway late at night. One of the group discovers that the shop door is not locked. He tries to persuade the rest to enter the shop with him to see what is inside. An argument ensues.

A passenger travelling by train with a friend becomes engaged in conversation with two football 'fans' in the compartment. Later the 'fans' become high-spirited, remove the bulbs from their sockets and, amidst much hilarity, toss them out of the window. What happens?

6. Examples of situations that will give the children some

practical experience of how to deal with social conventions.

   Ordering a meal in a restaurant.
   Answering a telephone.
   Asking a girl for a dance.
   Being interviewed for a job.
   Introducing a friend to one's headmaster.
   Showing a visitor round the school.
   Telephoning a distant relative and thanking him for an unexpected gift.
   Apologising to your neighbour because your dog has dug up his favourite rose bush.
   Making a complaint to a local shopkeeper.
   Proposing a vote of thanks to your host.

BLOCKS 15-22   Movement and Speech together

BLOCK 15 — *Movement and speech together—crowd*
                        scenes

Objective

To present the children with simple crowd scenes likely to stimulate movement and speech—scenes in which they can gain confidence as individuals within a large group, and in which their individual responsibilities to the group are limited.

Activities

The teacher narrates a story which is acted by the children

as he narrates. (Section 1 of this book is a comprehensive example of this sort of approach.)

Setting up a stall on market day and beginning to sell your wares.

A busy railway station on Bank Holiday Monday.

Shopping in a large department store.

A medieval banquet.

An earthquake, or similar disaster.

A crowded beach at a holiday resort.

A native village.

A building site.

A busy factory.

A royal procession.

A laundry.

A zoo.

A hospital.

BLOCK 16 — *Introduction of incidents into crowd scenes to give simple plots*

Objective

To introduce incidents into the scenes in order to give some dramatic shape (plot), and to provide a common aim for all the participants.

Activities

To illustrate how this should be developed from block 15, we have taken a cross-section of the crowd scenes suggested in block 15, and added possible developments.

1. A market scene.

Possible developments:

A cyclist crashes into one of the stalls, scattering vegetables, etc., amongst the feet of the crowd.

A thief is discovered. He holds the angry crowd at bay with a knife. The situation is saved by a policeman who persuades the thief to give up his knife. The crowd disperses, discussing the incident.

A messenger arrives and informs the crowd that a royal procession is on its way. The excited people line up and cheer the procession through.

As the afternoon draws to a close a messenger from the town hall arrives and informs the stall-holders that their rents are to be raised. An immediate meeting is held. A delegation is chosen, and leaves to protest to the mayor. The remaining stall-holders, now thoroughly dispirited, pack up their stalls and leave.

Gala day, during which the mayor and his retinue visit each stall in turn to judge a stall-dressing competition.

2. A railway station.
Possible developments:

A special holiday-makers' train fails to stop at the station, or arrives at the wrong platform, and leaves before most of the holiday-makers have realised the fact.

Arrival of the royal train.

Police arrive at the station looking for a spy who is believed to be carrying secret documents in his luggage.

A circus train arrives and begins to unload.

Happy holiday-makers have their spirits dampened when a funeral procession arrives with a coffin to be loaded onto their train.

3. A medieval banquet.
Possible developments:

> A herald arrives with a declaration of war.
> The lord of the manor drinks poisoned wine.
> A fire breaks out amongst the rushes on the floor.
> A witch arrives, is scorned, and lays a curse upon all present.
> Jugglers and tumblers arrive to entertain the guests.

4. A crowded beach.
Possible developments:

> A Punch and Judy man arrives and sets up his booth.
> A boat capsizes near the beach, and a human chain is formed to rescue the victims.
> Parents lose a small child. The news gradually spreads until everyone is involved.
> A sudden storm breaks. Holiday-makers beat a hasty retreat in search of shelter.
> A shark is sighted. Frightened parents hurriedly retrieve their children from the water's edge.

5. A busy factory.
Possible developments:

> One of the workers has an accident.
> Redundancy is threatened. The shop steward holds an immediate meeting to decide upon a course of action.
> An outside-broadcast team arrives with cameras, and sets about interviewing the workers.
> The automatic fire sprinkler system is triggered off by accident. This in turn sets off the burglar alarm.

The manager brings round a time-and-motion-study team. They are given a very cold reception. When they leave a meeting is held.

6. A native village.
Possible developments:

White explorers arrive unexpectedly. In order to win the confidence of the natives they offer them presents.

The village chief is dying. Unexpectedly a white man arrives at the village and cures him. A celebration is held.

Two natives have an argument. A ritual fight to the death is arranged and watched by the entire village.

A war party returns to the village carrying their dead chief. A ritual burial takes place, after which the witch doctor proclaims the dead chief's son as the new leader.

BLOCKS 17 – 20 — *Development of plays*

As shown in Fig. 3, page 128, the work is now divided into two streams, both leading towards group improvisation. In blocks 18 and 20 the children begin to take the responsibility for making up their own stories or plays, based on crowd situations already explored. In blocks 17 and 19 the teacher controls the plots more tightly, taking the opportunity to ensure that the children cover a sufficiently wide range in the work, and do not, for example, base play after play on bank robberies. As in Section 3, blocks 18 and 20 will be dealt with first.

BLOCK 18 — *Plays made by class discussion from given crowd situations*

Objective

To develop class plays based upon the interaction of various groups or crowds, so that the children, now working in smaller groups, have to take a greater part of the responsibility for ensuring that the group action is consistent with the agreed story. The individual child is no longer able to lose himself quite so easily in the crowd. Thus his individual responsibility towards the group is being developed (group sensitivity). He begins to appreciate that the welfare of the group is more important than his own personal needs and desires. The ultimate aim is that the child shall form the habit of using his talents for the good of the group rather than for his personal glorification.

Activities

As the development of these stories will depend upon class discussion, it is impossible to do more than suggest how the work can be tackled, and give a few ideas for crowd scenes which may be drawn upon to develop stories.

The development of a story from crowd scenes might go something like this:

"We've done several crowd scenes during the last few weeks. Can anyone remember any of them?"

"The fire of London, sir."

"The earthquake one."

"The market stalls."

"That one about the fishermen mending their nets."

"The prisoners of war, sir."

"Going to Blackpool on the train."

"The one about the coronation."

"Good. Now let's choose two or three of them and see if we can make up a play about them."

Practically all the crowd scenes will be chosen by one child or another. Give as many children as possible the opportunity of explaining what it was they particularly liked about the scenes of their choice, and if necessary steer the class towards a final choice of those scenes that you think will be most fruitful. Supposing that 'The laundry', 'The concentration camp' and 'The fishermen on the quayside' are eventually chosen, the story might be built up as follows:

"Right. Now, where is the play going to start?"

"In a concentration camp."

"Why?"

"Because we can have an escape."

"That's a good idea. Where's the camp going to be, in England or in Germany?"

"England."

"That means that we shall have German prisoners escaping?"

"Yes."

"All right. How are the prisoners going to escape?"

"Dig a tunnel."

"Cut through the wire."

"Clobber all the guards."

"Let's have them digging a tunnel, like the miners in that play we did the week before last. What are they going to do once they are clear of the camp?"

"Get a boat."

"Don't forget that they will still be wearing German uniforms."

"They could steal English uniforms from the laundry."

"That's a good idea."

. . . and so the discussion continues until the story is worked out. The class is then divided into three groups: the prisoners, the laundry workers and the fishermen. They are sent off to various parts of the hall to arrange the details of their particular parts of the story, e.g., the prisoners' group decides how many are to be prisoners, how many are to be guards, whether any prisoners are to be recaptured, and where the tunnel is to be located. Meanwhile the teacher goes from group to group helping and advising where necessary. When the groups are ready a first run-through can be attempted, those groups not required to participate at any one time watching the other groups with a view to offering constructive criticism. And so the work progresses until both the children and the teacher are satisfied with the results.

Below are some suggestions for crowd scenes from which class plays can be built:

An old-age pensioners' outing to Margate.
A mountaineering expedition.
A motor-cycling club visits a historic castle.
A scout camp.
A works outing to the seaside.
Putting up decorations for a party.
A jury attempting to reach a verdict.
A foreign delegation visiting a motor-car factory.
A team of Australian cane cutters at work.

Convicts working in a quarry.

Archaeologists excavating a Roman villa.

Druids performing a ceremony.

Sheep-shearers at work in New Zealand.

Arab merchants arriving at an oasis.

Building a pyramid.

A coachload of holiday-makers stranded on a lonely mountain road.

Families of gypsies helping during the hop-picking season.

BLOCK 20 — *Group plays made up by children from given crowd situations*

Objective

To encourage the children to develop and act their own group plays based on given crowd situations. Once they have proved themselves capable of organising their various groups to work out a part of an agreed story for a class play, they can be presented with the responsibility for organising and developing their own group plays based on crowd situations.

Activities

This work is very similar to that in block 9, page 86, but whereas in block 9 it is developed by enlarging pair situations, here it is developed by narrowing crowd scenes. Between them these two blocks represent the introductory work to most forms of group improvisation. Obviously use can be made of all the crowd situations previously mentioned. We have selected a few of these situations to show possible ways in which they can be developed into group plays.

1. Situation: An airport.

Establish the general atmosphere of an airport as a class crowd scene. The class is then divided into groups, and offered one of the following suggestions to develop:

A passenger finds himself stranded with no money or ticket. He attempts to approach a celebrity he recognises in the airport lounge.

A passenger picks up the wrong suitcase by mistake. He opens it to find three shrunken heads!

A fanatic tries to assassinate a well-known political figure arriving at the airport.

A refugee attempts to persuade the authorities to let him into the country.

The airport medical officer informs passengers that one of them is believed to be a smallpox carrier.

2. Situation: A zoo.

An announcement is made that a lion has disappeared. A small boy is discovered playing with it.

A chimpanzee spits in an elderly lady's face. She complains to the keeper.

An elephant removes an elderly gentleman's hat.

A small boy loses his white mouse in the reptile house.

A small girl gets her head stuck between some bars.

11 'Twas brillig; and the slithy toves
   Did gyre and gimble in the wabe.'

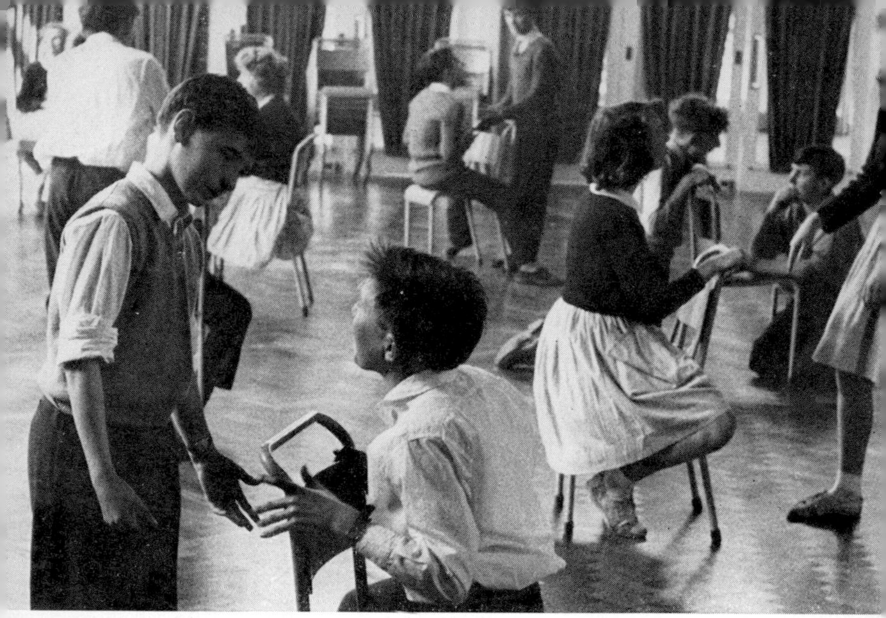

12 '. . . but look, I've got to get to Manchester tonight.'

14 '. . . and you pull this chromium-plated stopper bar.'

13 The flea trainers compare results.

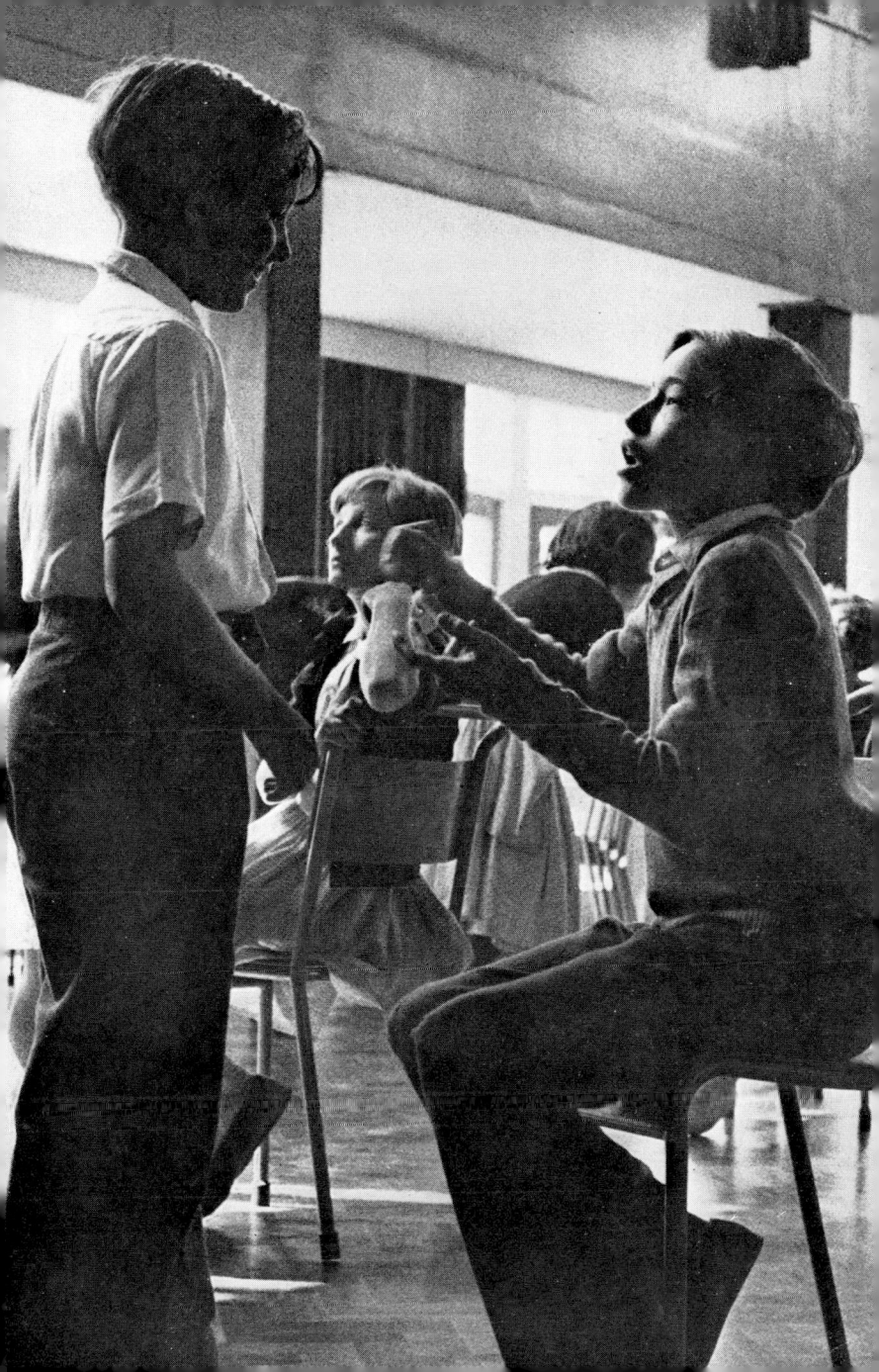

15 'Out!' I said, 'l.b.w.!'

16 Commuters.

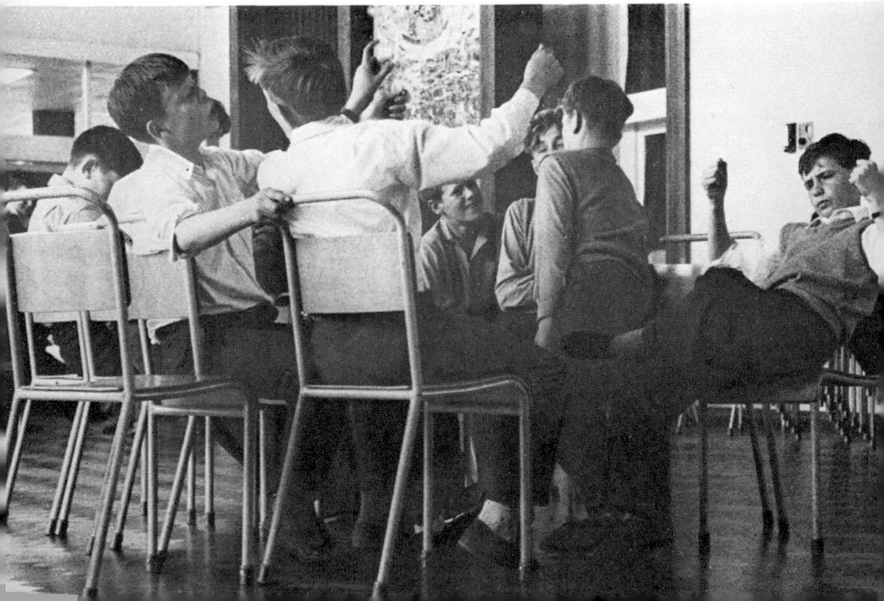

3. Situation: A fairground.

A customer complains that the rifles on the shooting range are 'fixed'.

The big wheel breaks down, leaving two very frightened old ladies in the top chair.

A customer keeps winning at the darts stall.

The fortune-teller's tent.

A headmaster discovers one of his pupils in charge of the one-arm bandits.

4. Situation: A youth club.

The club leader introduces a new member. He appears to be very 'posh', and owns a flashy sports car.

A girl loses a valuable watch.

The bully of the club deliberately treads on the ball during a table tennis match.

A local café proprietor arrives to complain about the behaviour of certain members of the club.

An old member reappears who, it is rumoured, has won £75,000 on the football pools.

5. Situation: A hospital.

A group of relatives gathers round a patient's bed. He has had an operation on his eyes and the bandages are about to be removed.

Just before the doctor's rounds it is discovered that a patient is missing. Hurried enquiries are made.

A new patient arrives. A policeman sits by his bed. Various rumours begin to circulate.

A foreigner, who speaks no English, arrives at the out-patients' department. He unsuccessfully attempts to explain what is wrong. Other well-meaning patients try to assist.

The fire alarm is accidentally set off in the middle of the night.

BLOCK 17 — *Improvised class plays based on teacher's suggestions*

Objective

To introduce the children to the idea of a more tightly-knit plot with some real dramatic shape, by means of class plays based on the teacher's suggestions.

Activities

Whereas it is relatively easy to think up simple situations, a good story is far more difficult to evolve, especially one that is suitable for use as a class play. However, the teacher need not rely entirely upon his own imagination. Current affairs and newspaper stories—riots, train accidents, royal visits, etc.—often provide useful material. But by far the most abundant sources are history and literature. Through these the children are not only introduced to worthwhile stories but, by enacting them, are given a much deeper insight into our heritage.

In making use of established stories the children should be given only a brief, bold outline, so that they are free to create their own detail through acting (see page 34). Themes should be chosen which either have sufficient characters already, or which can be easily adapted to cater for all the class. The following should prove useful.

1. Christopher Columbus.
   His departure—sailors, wives, royal procession, crowd and Columbus.
   His landing—Columbus, sailors and Indians.
   His return—Columbus, sailors, captured Indians, waiting crowds and royalty.

2. The Pied Piper of Hamelin.
   (This can either be done as a play in its own right, or to a narrator.)
   —Pied Piper, citizens, servants, lords and ladies, children and rats.

3. The Banquet scene from *Macbeth*.
   —servants, noblemen, Macbeth, Lady Macbeth, murderers and Banquo's ghost.

4. Oliver Twist.
   Oliver is suspected of having picked Mr. Brownlow's pocket.
   —Mr. Brownlow, the Dodger, Oliver, a policeman and crowd.

5. Jonah and the whale.
   —Jonah, Captain, sailors, the citizens of Nineveh, and a group of children to represent the whale.

6. Florence Nightingale at Scutari.
   —Florence, Mr. Bamford, nurses, doctors, priests and wounded soldiers.

7. Dr. Barnardo takes Lord Shaftesbury to see the orphan children of London sleeping on the roof-tops.

   —Barnardo, Lord Shaftesbury and some friends, ragged children.

8. The Jackdaw of Rheims.

   —The Cardinal, Jackdaw, assorted servants and guests.

9. The Crucifixion.

   —Jesus, soldiers, Mary and a crowd.

10. Useful material can be found almost anywhere, provided it is suitably edited. Some sources are:

   Three Plays for the Open Stage by BRIAN WAY.
   Pinocchio by BRIAN WAY.
   Great Expectations and many other books by DICKENS.
   Legends of King Arthur.
   Robin Hood.
   Stories from *The Odyssey* and *The Iliad*, translated by E. V. RIEU.
   The Bible, e.g., Noah and the Flood; Elijah and the Prophets of Baal; The Prodigal Son, etc.
   The Canterbury Tales, e.g., The Pardoner's Tale; The Nun's Priest's Tale: modernised version by NEVILL COGHILL.
   Treasure Island and *Kidnapped* by R. L. STEVENSON.
   Emil and the Detectives by ERICH KÄSTNER.
   The Tinder Box by HANS ANDERSEN.
   The Wizard of Oz by FRAMT BAUM.
   The Wooden Horse by ERIC WILLIAMS.
   The War of the Worlds by H. G. WELLS.
   Quatermass by NIGEL KNEALE.

BLOCK 19 — *Group plays based on teacher's suggestions*

Objective

To give the children, now that they are capable of working together harmoniously in small groups, the opportunity of developing and acting plays based on suggestions and hints from the teacher.

Activities

The teacher can approach this work from two angles: he may either offer the children a single starting-point such as an object, a sentence, a location or a number of characters, or he may offer them the simple outline of a plot. There are numerous examples under block 12 on page 88 for the first approach (where the emphasis is on group story-making rather than group story-acting or improvisation). The second approach needs some care in the choice of material. It is important to select situations that have some definite story, and do not simply rely upon the clever interplay of dialogue. This enables the teacher to present his suggestions as clear-cut anecdotes. Below are listed a few examples of the kind of material likely to be useful.

> *In the Zone* by EUGENE O'NEILL.
> The witch scenes in *Macbeth*.
> The mutiny scene on board Christopher Columbus' ship.
> The mime scene from *Hamlet*.
> The Good Samaritan.

Other sources of suitable material:

> *Oliver Twist*—CHARLES DICKENS.

Peer Gynt—IBSEN.

Peter Grimes—GEORGE CRABBE.

The Nosebag—LOUIS MACNEICE.

The Second Shepherd's Play, and other miracle and mystery plays.

Alice in Wonderland—LEWIS CARROLL.

The Blitz Kids—E. MORDAUNT.

The Black Marigold—GILLIAN BELL.

The Sword and the Stone—T. H. WHITE.

Tom Sawyer and *Huckleberry Finn*—MARK TWAIN.

The Hobbit—J. R. R. TOLKIEN.

Three Men in a Boat—JEROME K. JEROME.

Moonfleet—J. MEADE FAULKNER.

The field from which to select scenes or incidents for group improvisations is vast, but whatever is chosen it is important to remember that, if the improvisation is to have any real dramatic impact, it must contain mental and/or physical conflict leading to a climax, and the eventual release of tension.

BLOCK 21 — *Group improvisations*

Objective

For the children to take the responsibility for choosing, developing and acting their own group plays. This is in fact the climax of the drama course so far (see also block 22, page 112, which bridges the gap between drama and theatre).

Activities

The material for improvisation will now be chosen and

developed by the children in their various groups. This will result in group requirements being so diverse that the main problem will become one of organisation.

Each group will need to have somebody responsible for production, stage management, lighting, and possibly 'props' and sound-effects as well. By this time the most likely children will have shown themselves, and their abilities will be generally recognised. In some cases one child may be doing two or three of these jobs—as well as acting in the play.

The children will need longer to prepare and rehearse their plays. Also, if they are going to make use of lighting, sound, a rostrum and/or the stage, etc., they will need time to arrange the equipment. To mount and perform a short group improvisation, after it has been rehearsed, may well take the best part of a period. Under these circumstances it is usually impracticable for more than one group play to be presented per lesson. There needs, therefore, to be some sort of rota system whereby the groups take it in turns to present their plays, leaving sufficient time afterwards for a discussion on the merits of the play and its presentation. Each lesson could well consist of a general rehearsal for all groups except the one due to present its play. This group could be setting up the necessary equipment for its production. The pattern of these lessons can be varied from time to time by the teacher giving specific instruction on the technical aspects of presentation, following this up by various tests of competence (practical or written).

The vital factor in all this work is that the children must, and at this stage certainly should, be able to work together harmoniously, not only as individuals within a group, but also as groups within a class. Without this sort of co-operation the work is impossible. With so many children doing so many different things at the same time the teacher must be able to trust them to behave sensibly. From time to time snags will arise, and the teacher will feel that his trust has been betrayed, but he must be prepared to run this risk. He can, however, minimise the risk by establishing certain commonsense rules.

1. Only the group about to present its play is allowed to use the necessary equipment.
2. No child is allowed to use any equipment unless qualified to do so (test of competence). In this way it is possible to compile a list of 'qualified' electricians, sound-effects men, scene shifters, etc.
3. If, during rehearsal time, any insoluble snag or argument arises, the 'producer' of the group contacts the teacher at once. In this way the teacher is able to keep in contact with the groups.

Finally, the teacher should establish the idea that working in this way, and being allowed to use the technical facilities, is a special privilege, and that anyone found abusing it will have the privilege withdrawn.

BLOCK 22 — *Polished group and class improvisations*

Objectives

1. To help the children acquire the discipline necessary to continue working at an improvisation after the initial excitement of creation has worn off.
2. To reveal the fresh satisfaction that comes when, after

the grind of rehearsal, an improvisation acquires clear
dramatic shape and full impact.
3. To prepare the children for production (see also pages
135 and 149).

As the children become accustomed to criticising their
own plays and those of other groups, the idea of drama as
something to be communicated to others arises naturally.
Drama begins to merge into theatre, and the bridge between
the two is the polished improvisation. Successful communication involves considering and selecting the right
material, and moulding it into an effective dramatic pattern.
To maintain the pattern once it has been established, some
form of written record will become essential. This may
take the form of either a scenario, or a simple script, setting
out the important lines, cues and locations. Finally, the most
effective way of showing the work must be decided. This
will entail considering and selecting the best techniques for
showing to an audience (theatre in the round? stage? lighting? varying levels? sound effects? etc.).

Activities

These may be chosen and developed by the children, as in
blocks 20 and 21 on pages 103 and 110, or by the class under
the teacher's leadership, as in block 17 on page 106, but however a particular improvisation is initiated, the children will
need a considerable amount of tactful help from the teacher
if they are to achieve a satisfying result in a reasonably short
time.

With an ambitious improvisation it may be that, at the
final stage of polishing, the class will look to the teacher as
its producer.

H

FIG. 2. Example of a typical scenario sheet evolved through polishing a dance improvisation based on the colour problem.

SCENE I

Cue	Light	Sound
1. 3 seconds after the house lights have faded out.	Lights fade in on blocks A to reveal white youths miming a knife fight.	Record of *Big Fella* fades in slowly.
2. White youths leap down from blocks A.	Lights fade up on solitary negro asleep on block B.	
3. White youths see negro and slowly move towards him.	Lights on blocks A fade out gradually.	
4. Youths surround negro, who has a large hat pulled down over his eyes.		
5. One youth creeps up on negro and takes his hat. Negro wakes up. Youths play with the hat, trying to tempt the negro away from his block.		
6. Youths eventually stamp on hat and move back to blocks A.	Lights on blocks A fade back in as youths return.	
7. Youths reach blocks A.	Lights on blocks A fade out slowly.	Music fades out.

Cue	Light	Sound
8. Negro slowly and sadly recovers his hat.		Record of *Black Brown and Beige* (Duke Ellington) fades in.
9. Negro sits on block B looking at hat.	Lights on block B fade slowly.	Music fades out with lights.

In addition to fictional themes, the following, tackled as documentaries, all lend themselves to polished improvisations:

> The training of a policeman (policewoman).
> Refugees.
> The problem of famine relief.
> The history of smuggling.
> Women's emancipation.
> The exploration of space.
> The growth of the Welfare State.
> The history of dance.
> Primitive rituals in modern society.
> The development of medical science.
> How a newspaper is produced.
> The development of communications.
> The development of transport.
> The growth of the trade union movement.
> Contesting a by-election.
> Making a film.
> The probation service.
> The work of UNESCO.
> How the law works.

5 Planning a drama lesson

As was emphasised earlier in this book, drama work has been divided into various blocks only because this seemed to be the simplest way of rationalising and grouping together the different aspects. It should now, for example, be an easy matter for the teacher who wants to stimulate speech at some point in the course to turn to a few notes on the theory (Section 3, page 45), and some practical examples to back it up (Section 4, page 82). It is *not* our intention that the teacher should rigidly undertake his practical work in small self-contained compartments. A class would soon become bored, for example, with a lesson based entirely on block 2, page 69 (imaginative movement individually and in pairs), consisting simply of the examples given, strung together with no apparent progression.

The teacher must guard against his lesson degenerating into a series of exercises. The real content of drama is *story*, in which mood, movement, character, speech, etc., all combine. The teacher must build towards story.

The aim of any lesson, even if taken directly from that given at the head of a block, will usually pre-suppose the need for work from a selection of related blocks.

As an example, the aim at the head of block 16, page 96 (introduction of incidents into crowd scenes to give simple plots), can only be furthered if some background work is done at the beginning of the lesson. Such work might be drawn from any related blocks and might well include some story-making (block 10, page 88), speech work in pairs and groups (block 8, page 84) and certainly some work on crowd scenes covered by block 15, page 95. The lesson could conclude by moving towards the class play (block 18, page 100).

Every drama lesson must give the children a feeling of progression, and the teacher should be prepared to move from one block to another to get this progression.

Children will feel no sense of achievement unless their work builds into something worthwhile. They are not prepared to wait four years for this: it must be more immediately obvious.

The teacher should try always to keep in mind the remarks made at the beginning of Section 3 regarding the simultaneous progression of the three main types of activity (page 40).

More details of the thought and preparation necessary are given in the following three examples of different types of lessons. Although each is based upon a specific block, use is made of material from related blocks, either to begin or end the lesson.

Using the system of blocks in Fig. 3 to prepare a drama lesson

1. BASING A LESSON ON BLOCK 3—IMPROVISED CLASS PLAYS TO MUSIC

This particular example would probably extend over three lessons. The first lesson might be approached as follows:

Objective

To give the children the opportunity of contributing their individual or small group efforts towards a class activity. (See block 3, page 72.)

Main activity

A dance drama based on the fire of London.

Introduction

A general warm-up to music (block 2, page 69), selecting movement activities likely to be useful in the dance drama.

1. In pairs: rescuing belongings from a fire. ('The Dance of King Kastchei' from *The Firebird*.)
2. In pairs: rescuing an injured friend from a smoke-filled room. ('Baba Yaga' from *Pictures at an Exhibition*.)
3. In pairs: two people frantically trying to save a heavy chest of valuables from an upstairs bedroom. (Music as in 1. above.)
4. Groups of people passing buckets from hand to hand in an effort to put out a fire. (The last section of *The Sorcerer's Apprentice*.)
5. People returning to their burnt-out homes after the fire to salvage what belongings they can. ('Elihu's Dance of Youth and Beauty' from *Job*.)

Beginning the story

1. A general discussion on the fire of London, bringing out such interesting historical details as the type of fire engine (if any) that might have been used; the narrowness of the streets; the combustible nature of the build-

ings; the sort of clothes worn and how they might have hampered movement; water sources; etc.

2. Some practice at being Londoners going about their normal business in pairs and small groups.

3. In this situation the fire alarm is raised—what would the immediate reactions be? Do some practical work on this to explore various possibilities.

4. A general run-through of the fire of London scene:

   (a) Londoners going about their normal business.

   (b) The fire alarm is raised, and the people endeavour to put the fire out and rescue what they can of their belongings.

   (c) The fire is over. The people return to their burnt-out homes to salvage anything left.

Conclusion

The teacher holds a general discussion with the class about the work they have done, and explains to them that next week they will be rebuilding London. He asks them to find out what they can about the buildings of those days: how were they constructed, etc.?

2. A LESSON BASED ON BLOCK 9—SPEECH SITUATIONS IN PAIRS LEADING TO GROUP PLAYS

Objective

To build up group plays from simple speech situations in pairs by adding characters and incidents.

Main activity

An old lady loses her spectacles down a drain when she trips.

Without them she is almost blind. A passer-by comes to her aid. Add to this a policeman, his suspicious inspector, a drain cleaner, and a valuable necklace.

Introduction

A number of speech situations in pairs (block 8, page 84) as a warm-up and a general lead into the main activity.

1. Directing a stranger in a large city.
2. Directing a slightly deaf old lady.
3. A policeman directs a slightly deaf old lady.
4. A helpful stranger assists a small boy who had his hand stuck in a grating.
5. A blind man asks a passing stranger to help him find a particular shoe shop, the name of which he has forgotten.
6. A policeman is discovered eating sandwiches on duty by his inspector.
7. A drain cleaner endeavours to remove an Alsatian dog which is asleep on top of the drain he wishes to inspect.

Beginning the story

1. In pairs: an old lady stumbles over a grating and her glasses fall into it. Being unable to see very well without them, she blunders into a passer-by as she is searching for them. She enlists his help.
2. In threes: add to this situation a helpful policeman.
3. In fours: a suspicious police inspector appears on the scene to discover the policeman on his hands and knees in the gutter.
4. A jolly drain cleaner arrives to discover the stranger, the policeman and the inspector all on their hands and knees, groping about in the drain with their sleeves rolled up.

The old lady is hovering round hopefully. The drain cleaner agrees to help.

5. A valuable necklace is discovered. There is an argument. What happens? Each group decides for itself what the conclusion to the story is to be. The whole story is run through.

Conclusion

A general discussion is held on the various conclusions.

3. A LESSON BASED ON BLOCK 15—MOVEMENT AND SPEECH TOGETHER—CROWD SCENES

Objective

To present the children with a simple crowd scene likely to stimulate movement and speech—a scene in which they can gain confidence as individuals within a large group, where their individual responsibilities to the group are very limited.

Main activity

A crowded beach (block 15, page 95).

Introduction

A general warm-up session on movement, allowing the children to introduce speech if they wish to (block 1, page 66, and block 7, page 82).

1. Individually: imagine that the floor of the hall is a sandy beach. Make a pattern with your footprints to cover as much of it as possible. (*Roulette* by RUSS CONWAY.)

2. Individually: exploring a rock pool and collecting any interesting items. Get the children to suggest possible objects. (The opening of *The Sorcerer's Apprentice*.)
3. Individually: building a sand castle which eventually collapses unexpectedly. Use a cymbal for the build-up and crash.
4. In pairs: playing with a beach-ball. (*Little Rock Getaway* —LES PAUL.)
5. In pairs: changing into your bathing costume with the help of a towel, and joining an impatient friend at the water's edge.
6. In pairs: a deck-chair attendant wakes up a bad-tempered old man to ask him if he has a ticket for his deck-chair. He *has*!
7. A beach photographer pesters a local resident.

Development

The teacher narrates a series of activities for the children to do, starting with the arrival at the beach. (See Section 1, page 13, for a representative example of this approach.)

Holiday-makers arrive at the beach on a sunny day. They select a suitable spot, get changed, and dash into the water. Suddenly a storm breaks, they hurry back to their belongings, collect them and dash for shelter under the pier. The storm passes and they return to the beach to eat their sandwiches. After tea they play games, take a walk on the pier, search rock pools, build sand castles, etc., etc. As the sun sets they gather together their belongings and trudge wearily off to the bus station to join the rapidly growing queue.

Conclusion

The teacher may discuss with the children any possible developments, what parts they particularly enjoyed and why, and what they are going to do next week.

Alternative development

The children select various characters for themselves (beach photographer, deck-chair attendant, fisherman, pier manager, families on holiday, etc.), and the scene begins with all going about their business. When the children show signs of losing interest the teacher can either introduce a few incidents to stimulate fresh interest (a storm, a boat capsizing, a Punch and Judy show, etc.), leading into block 16, page 96, or, if he feels that the situation is played out, he can simply stop the scene and start work on a new crowd situation.

6   Practical organisation

Drama of the kind described in this book needs space. To be realistic, it is essential to have a hall or gymnasium in which to work, or at least a large class-room where desks can be moved out of the way quickly and easily. It is important to clear such things as vases of flowers, so that the children and the teacher may feel free to use the space and concentrate upon the lesson, without the worry of possible damage.

Equipment

Check that the equipment to be used is at hand and in working order before the lesson begins. A whole lesson can be ruined by discovering at the crucial moment that someone has changed the gramophone plug, or that no sound comes from the loudspeaker because one has forgotten to switch on the amplifier. Time spent in stimulating a class to react to a piece of music will be wasted if there is a wait of even fifteen seconds while the amplifier warms up. The atmosphere has gone, together with the teacher's self-confidence! Similarly, nothing can be more disconcerting than the quick dash to the staff room to collect a forgotten record.

Noise

If the children are to be encouraged to speak freely, and the hall is, from time to time, to be filled with music for movement work, it must be accepted that a reasonable amount of noise is essential. What reasonable teacher would expect a music lesson to be conducted quietly?

It is imperative that other members of the staff do not merely tolerate the noise, grudgingly, but come to appreciate why it is necessary.

The considerate drama teacher can at least do something to minimise noise:

1. Make sure that all doors are shut.
2. Do not open windows adjacent to or opposite classrooms.
3. Experiment with positions for the loudspeaker until one is found that lets the least amount of noise escape from the hall.

Staff relations

By its very nature, drama is an easy target for uninformed and destructive criticism. On first sight, many people view it with suspicion. The drama teacher should take every opportunity to explain to other members of staff what he is doing, and encourage them to view the subject with an open mind. At the very least, many petty annoyances can be avoided by a little consideration and forethought. The following commonsense points will obviously help:

1. Ensure that classes always enter and leave the hall in an orderly fashion—"Just because we have had a drama lesson it doesn't mean that we can be seals all the way to the science lab."
2. Give the children the chance to 'wind down' at the end of a lesson, so that they can come back to reality before they

leave the hall. The teacher who fails to do this will most certainly antagonise those unfortunate members of staff who have to cope with an unsettled and rowdy class afterwards.

3. Always leave time at the end of a session for the children to change, so that they are not late for the next lesson.

4. Be prepared to avoid the more noisy activities in special circumstances, i.e., examinations.

5. Avoid creating extra work for other people by failing to tidy up afterwards.

DISCIPLINE

The well-disciplined class is the one which acknowledges, accepts and works within the framework of certain rules. The only basic difference between discipline in class-room subjects and discipline in drama is that the rules are different not that they are non-existent. When we are working in drama we *do* speak and we *do* move about freely.

Many people falsely assume that because the children are allowed to speak and move freely in drama there is no discipline. This is not so. Providing the children are doing the work asked of them, approaching it with sincerity and absorption, and paying close attention to the teacher when asked, they are both well disciplined and controlled. However, as this is a new kind of discipline, it is imperative that the teacher makes quite clear the sort of behaviour he expects from the beginning.

For example, as it will obviously be necessary to stop the work from time to time in order to discuss it, or to pass on instructions, some convention (other than shouting one's head off) must be established. In early lessons, while the children are learning to respond to sound, they can also be taught that the correct response to a hand clap is to stand or sit quietly and pay attention to the teacher. Similarly they never begin an activity until told to do so, or disturb another group which is still working, merely because they have finished first. This is an important aspect of their training, and is essential if the work is to run smoothly. If a sceptical headmaster walks into one of your drama lessons, there is no better way of convincing him that the situation is under control than by obtaining complete stillness and silence by one clap of the hands!

ESTABLISHING A ROUTINE

It is essential, as in all teaching, that a routine be established so that the children know what is expected of them. The routine will obviously vary according to the conditions under which the teacher is working, but definite decisions should be reached on the following points:

What to wear

If conditions permit, the children should change into the sort of clothing which lends itself to free and vigorous movements. This is particularly necessary for girls who are otherwise unduly hampered by their skirts (if they have a special kit for dancing this will probably be very suitable).

If changing facilities are not available—the usual case—it will have to be a matter of simply removing jackets and ties.

Ideally the children should work in bare feet or 'pumps', not stockinged feet which easily slip.

The important thing is to make a definite ruling about the kit to be worn, and then to stick to it. This has an obvious practical value as well as a psychological one. It not only ensures an atmosphere of 'off jackets and down to work', but also the feeling that drama is something rather special and that an extra effort is called for. In the early stages it is advisable to make as definite a routine as possible. The children should line up outside the hall, walk in quietly, change, find themselves an empty space on the floor, and relax. This may be modified later, as self-discipline is developed; the children can start warming up on their own before the lesson begins, thus saving time. If and when this becomes the accepted practice, the teacher can finish the lesson by suggesting a few ideas for the children to use during their warm-up the following week. Under these ideal conditions it may not even be necessary for them to line up before entering the hall.

At the end of the lesson the children should get into the habit of lining up quietly by the door as soon as they have changed. They should leave a drama lesson in the same way that they would any other.

Rules and regulations

It should be made quite clear to the children that they are expected to work within certain limits. These should be clearly defined in the form of a few simple rules, such as:

1. You may use chairs, but when moving them they must be lifted, not dragged.

2. Curtains and doors are to be left strictly alone—likewise the tape recorder, gramophone and records.
3. The stage is out of bounds without special permission.
4. Nobody else's property (satchels, scarves, etc.) is to be borrowed for a play without the permission of the owner.

Most of these rules are common sense, but it is wise to make them quite clear from the beginning. There is nothing more frustrating than to have to stop in full flight to extricate a small child from behind the curtains!

CREATING THE RIGHT ATMOSPHERE

Physical surroundings

In whatever surroundings the drama lesson takes place, a conscious attempt should be made to create the right physical atmosphere as an aid to stimulation and absorption.

Movement work will usually be more successful if a blackout can be arranged and spotlights used to give areas of light and shadow.

The children will not only gain confidence from this but will also tend to make use of the different intensities of light in their work. A variety of different levels can be achieved by the use of a few blocks.

The imagination can be stimulated by interesting objects and pictures displayed round the hall that may be used later for group plays. Even if only a bare class-room is available, at least some effort can be made to create a stimulating atmosphere, particularly if you can arrange to use the same room for all your drama lessons.

I

Gaining the children's confidence

It is essential for the children to have confidence in the drama teacher if they are to create sincerely. If they do not feel completely at ease there will be some aspects of the work that they will feel self-conscious about tackling in front of the teacher. They may be reluctant to display some of their childish fears or their delight in fantasy: reluctance to acknowledge fear will emphasise it, and reluctance to display pleasure will inhibit the imagination.

The drama teacher must, however, be aware of the dangers here. In gaining the child's confidence he may well become the only member of staff, or indeed the only adult in the child's life, in whom the child feels free to confide. This whole drama teacher/pupil relationship needs very tactful handling.

Sincerity and absorption

Child drama is based on sincere and absorbed participation. What the children show the teacher as an adult is of little importance. His concern is that their feelings and thoughts should be genuine. One of his most important tasks is to be able to recognise sincerity and absorption when he sees it. He must train himself to judge the children's work from this point of view. Until he can do this he will be handicapped by the fact that he will not be able to decide whether a particular activity has been successful, or whether it needs doing again from a fresh angle to increase sincerity and absorption.

Self-consciousness is the main enemy of sincerity and absorption. It is for this reason that so much emphasis is placed on gaining confidence in the early part of the course. If at any time the children appear to be unduly self-conscious, it will usually be because the material is too sophisticated or because it is more suited to younger children. One cannot expect a group of first-year girls to become absorbed in the sort of work on social training covered in block 14 (page 92), any more than one can expect a group of fourth-year boys to tiptoe through the tulips chasing imaginary butterflies!

The teacher with imagination, a gift for vivid description and the ability to create mood and atmosphere with his voice, will have little difficulty in stimulating the response he is after. It is unrealistic to expect a sincerity and absorption without effective stimulation. The drama teacher should, therefore, make every effort to cultivate these gifts.

GENERAL TEACHING POINTS

1. Encourage active listening.
2. Never address the class until they are not only still but really attentive.
3. Remember that drama is a practical subject, and that the children will always prefer to do it rather than talk about it.
4. Make your instructions quite clear and vivid, but brief, and always check that the children have understood them before they begin the activity.
5. Make sure that every lesson has some real point or progression. Check that the children realise this at the end of the lesson, even if it is only to point out that they have been experimenting with fast and slow movement and how this will be developed next week.

6. If the activities you have chosen to achieve your lesson aim do not produce the result you had hoped for, be prepared to scrap them on the spot and try a fresh approach.

7. If the lesson shows signs of developing in a different direction to the one you had planned, do not be afraid to encourage and utilise this if there is obvious value in it. Always be prepared to modify your ideas according to the response.

8. Encourage the children to contribute their own ideas. Not only is this good for them, it also often helps you if you are stuck for a story!

9. Don't bully the shy child into participating. Let him take his own time, within reason.

10. Don't expect full participation from every child all the time. You won't get it.

11. Children who are a nuisance, and there will always be a few, should be dealt with as unobtrusively as possible so that the work of the rest of the class is not interrupted. Try to impress on the awkward children the need for tolerance: the fact that although they may not be particularly interested in the activity in hand, other children are, and should not be disturbed. If this does not work, give them something specific to do that limits their freedom. It could be simply sitting down and making a few notes about the work in progress.

12. Be ready to deal firmly and immediately, and if necessary in public, with the child likely to interfere with the lesson by serious anti-social behaviour. Explain to him and to the rest of the class the reason for this action.

13. Try to get across to the children the idea that you expect them to be able to work without close supervision. Make a point of being surprised and disappointed if they let you down. This is particularly important in group work. You cannot be in six places at once.

14. Work the children hard: do not give them the chance to become bored. If, for example, they are working on group plays, create a sense of purpose by limiting the time allowed to decide upon the story to as little as two or three minutes.

15. Don't overwork a situation. Train yourself to know when the children have got as much as they are likely to get out of it, and then leave it and go on to something new.

16. Don't break the continuity of an activity by interrupting it without very good reason, as the children may find it difficult to recapture the atmosphere.

Starting drama with third- and fourth-years

This situation usually arises only when drama is first started in a school, and it would be stupid to deny that dealing with third- and fourth-year classes who have done no drama before can be a problem—at least at first. The inexperienced drama teacher would be well advised to concentrate on the lower end of the school. He will find the children more responsive, and less likely to take advantage of the inevitable mistakes he will make to begin with.

If, however, you are faced with a class of third- or fourth-year children who have never done drama before, bear the following points in mind:

They may appear truculent and unco-operative. This will probably be because they are apprehensive about what you may ask them to do and are frightened of being made to look fools.

Do not aggravate this apprehension by throwing them in at the deep end. Eagerly exclaiming, "Take off your shoes and socks, boys!" will usually result in either blank incredulity or open hostility—particularly from those with dirty feet! Likewise, the suggestion, "Find yourselves an empty space on the floor," will only lead to an embarrassed shuffle towards the security of the radiators.

You must be prepared to consider their age and maturity (or at least their feelings of maturity), and break them in gently. Allay their fears by starting with the sort of activity they are used to, such as play reading. From this it should be possible to lead into an improvisation based on a dramatic scene from the play (ostensibly so that they do not have to worry about learning lines).

Later, as they gain confidence, you might be able to tackle some vigorous movement work based on stylised sword fighting or wrestling, strictly controlled by numbers or drum beats. Alternatively, the problem of turning the improvisation into a piece of film might be attempted. Whatever is tackled must appear to be obviously adult and, for the boys, manly.

7 Using drama as an approach to scripted plays

Whilst, as has previously been stated, drama is not directly concerned with theatre, it is undoubtedly an excellent grounding for acting and has a great deal in common with Stanislavsky's ideas. Certainly, for children, there is no better approach to scripted work than through improvisation.

As the children grow older, those who become interested in acting can utilise their experience in school drama, and use it as an approach to theatre. If their drama course has been successful they will have learned sensitivity, absorption and sincerity—the most important aspects of the actor's mental make-up. Apart from this they should also have mastered the physical skills of speech and movement. They must now learn to adapt these skills to the needs of theatre (projection) and to interpret a script with the help of the producer.

Approaching scripted work through improvisation

There are two possible ways of tackling this work. Either the actors can be presented with a clear and definite outline of a relevant extract from the play and asked to work on it as group improvisation (block 19, page 109), or they can be presented with a parallel situation involving the same emotional problems but in a different setting (they might be asked to explore a situation involving a fairground fortune-teller as a lead-in to the first witches' scene from *Macbeth*).

This enables the actor, from the beginning, to think in terms of character and situation rather than in terms of learning lines to 'say'. The script ceases to represent only words on a page to be learned; it becomes appreciated as a dramatic situation to be acted. This helps to overcome one of the most common faults in acting—the tendency to 'say' well-learned lines 'at' fellow actors, rather than to talk to other characters involved in a dramatic situation.

Approaching crowd scenes through improvisation

In many plays crowd scenes are lacking in content. They consist only of a few cryptic stage directions and one or two lines, which leave the rest of the crowd as purely decorative and often uninvolved bystanders. This results in the action becoming artificial and stilted, whereas a lively and absorbed crowd can add much to the pace and general atmosphere. Again, the best approach is through improvisation. In this way, the crowd are free to create and understand a genuine response to the situation. The producer then selects and rehearses the best aspects of this work (polished improvisation).

This is the natural approach for children who have done drama. They are quickly able to become involved and their training in group sensitivity enables them to discipline their responses to the requirements of the scene. It is worth noting that even people who have had no previous experience of improvisation will benefit from and enjoy this method of production.

There is no doubt that children with drama experience introduce a new freshness, sincerity and vitality into their theatre work, and it is right that the emphasis should be on these aspects rather than on the extremely difficult and sophisticated techniques of professional acting.

Forms of theatre for children's plays

In their drama lessons children will have established certain conventions:

1. Working on the floor rather than on the stage.
2. Making full use of space.
3. Varying levels by the use either of rostrum blocks, or of flowing on and off the stage.
4. Making use of sincerity and absorption, rather than costume and scenery, to create character and location.
5. Being unrestricted by the necessity to play to an audience on one particular side.

They will not have found these conventions limiting—rather the reverse. Any production with children should take this into account, not only because the children will feel happier working within the conventions that they are used to, but also because the conventions themselves offer more flexible and exciting forms of theatre.

Adults watching or producing a play done by children should not expect it to conform to the limited conventions of adult theatre. The more sophisticated adult approach of the 'box set' within the proscenium arch not only has obvious physical limitations, but demands difficult and exacting techniques which few amateur actors ever manage to master.

Plays for children should cater for at least some of the following needs:

1. Plots should be fast-moving and varied, and not merely 'watered-down' versions of sophisticated adult situations.
2. Elaborate sets should be avoided, and the atmosphere created with the help of a few well-chosen props, in the convention of the Elizabethan theatre.
3. Lighting and sound should be used both to create atmosphere and to link one scene with the next. They should be used as a positive aid to creating the illusion, rather than simply to light the actors' faces or cover up the sound of noisy scene shifters.
4. Imaginative use should be made of space and levels to create a variety of locations.
5. Do not be afraid to use a combination of floor space and stage. The actual size and shape of the floor space should be conditioned by the requirements of the play, and not by any preconceived ideas about theatre in the round, or for that matter by the size of the audience; the play can always be put on for another night if necessary.

By fulfilling these needs the productions will not only prove more exciting for the children, but provide the audience with a fresh and stimulating experience.

8 Appendix

RECORDED MUSIC[1]

Records are essential equipment. The choice of the best records to buy and use is important. Try to persuade the school to buy some for the sole use of the drama department. If you suddenly need creepy music to heighten an effect, it is no use having to send down to the music room for it! Often, although you prepare thoroughly, a certain piece of music will suddenly be just right and it must be to hand.

Modern microgroove records are expensive, so you are not likely to be able to buy very many. Take care of those you do buy. Although they are unbreakable, the grooves scratch easily, and dust and grit clinging to greasy fingerprints on the grooves will soon lead to pronounced crackle and hiss. There is nothing more irritating than trying to hear and respond to a quiet moment through the hiss and splutter of a damaged record.

Looking after records

1. Always keep them in their cases.
2. Handle by the edges (do not finger grooves).

[1] Although attempts are made to keep this section up-to-date with each reprinting, records are added or deleted from catalogues with increasing speed, making particular versions unobtainable, or better and perhaps cheaper versions suddenly obtainable. Readers are advised to check catalogue numbers before ordering. This particular list was revised in November 1967.

3. Frequently clean them with a proprietary cleaner (e.g. Emitex).
4. Try to avoid scratching them with the gramophone stylus if you have to start in the middle of a record.

Building up a stock

There are usually several different versions of a record available. Try to make sure that the one you buy does the job you intend; it is surprising how interpretations vary. That fast busy music you found so useful may lose much of its character when slowed down slightly by another conductor. The records listed below are those found to be most useful, not necessarily the ones most liked by the music critics![1]

Make sure that you are thoroughly familiar with your records. It helps to keep a note of the uses to which you can put the music you have available. Unless you know a lot about music, it may take some time to build up a comprehensive vocabulary of suitable material. It is only when you have trained yourself to recognise potentially useful music whenever you happen to hear it that you will begin to build up a library of useful material.

Buying records

Try to collect records to cover as many different moods as possible. Until you have done this you cannot afford the

[1] Whilst the remarks concerning the list of the most suitable interpretation still apply, many more 'bargain label' records are now available than when the book was first written. In these circumstances it seems unrealistic to recommend records costing £2, when useful versions can be obtained for a quarter of that price. Before buying cheap versions not listed in the following pages, it would be sensible to listen to them as they can sometimes be very disappointing.

luxury of buying a particular record solely because it has a short extract that you think might be useful for a dance drama. In practice a very few 'basic' records will cover most moods, and also give some opportunity for dance drama.

Basic types of music needed

1. Bright cheerful music to use for 'warm-up' activities, and to accompany some crowd scenes, e.g., railway station, shopping, etc.
2. Busy music for rush, panic, markets, etc.
3. Rhythmic music for early movement control and such things as machines and robots.
4. Processional music for royal occasions, banquets, etc.
5. Rough, tempestuous music for storms and battle scenes.
6. Frightening music.
7. 'Heavy', plodding music for lifting weights and strong exertion.
8. Stealthy music to use for movement control, burglars and creeping about.
9. Ethereal music for exploring caves and sinister activities.
10. Pastoral music for contemplative activities, woodlands, desert islands, etc.

It is possible to cover all these quite cheaply, but you will lack variety and eventually need to extend. The versions and couplings listed below will give you maximum coverage, and some additional material for the lowest cost.

Buying to a limit of £5

Time to Play—RUSS CONWAY (MFP 1096)

This collection of early recordings includes 'Side Saddle',

'Roulette' and 'Trampolina', and covers many aspects of note 1 above.

The Music of Leroy Anderson (Decca AH 118)

This invaluable record covers note 3 with: 'The Syncopated Clock', 'The Typewriter' and 'Jazz Pizzicato'. Other tracks cover aspects of notes 1 and 2.

Pictures at an Exhibition—MUSSORGSKY (Decca ACL 48)

This contains a wide variety of useful material, including:

busy music (2)—'Limoges'
heavy music (7)—'Catacombs', 'Gnomes' and 'Bydlo'
frightening music (6)—'The Hut on Fowls' Legs' and 'Catacombs'
pastoral music (10)—'Il Vecchio Castello'

Peter Grimes, Four Sea Interludes and Passacaglia—BENJAMIN BRITTEN (Decca ACL 162)

This covers note 5 with an excellent 'storm', and includes useful ethereal and quiet music, note 9. The Passacaglia could also provide a basis for a dance drama.

Trumpet Voluntary (Columbia SCD 2005)

This will cover the need for processional music, but is not ideal. For a little more money, a more useful record is available (see below).

'Mars'—from The Planets suite—HOLST (HMV 7P 203)

This particular version has real 'drive' and provides frightening music (6) and stealthy music (8). It is useful in that as it stands side two is short and simple enough to be used as an early dance drama. It might be more economical in the long run, however, to spend an extra five shillings on a cheap version of the whole suite (MFP 2014).

Peer Gynt—GRIEG (MAL 605)

This provides pastoral music (10) in 'Morning', and other possibilities including such things as a dance drama based on 'The Hall of the Mountain King'.

If slightly more than £5 can be spent, it is worth amending the list to include:

Music for Trumpet and Orchestra (Decca ACL-R 56) instead of the recording of *Trumpet Voluntary* suggested above.

On this record *Trumpet Tune and Air* provides a gloriously regal background, and there is a better version of *Trumpet Voluntary*.

The Sorcerer's Apprentice—DUKAS (Decca CEP 547)

There are many versions of this available, but this, with Georg Solti conducting the Israel Philharmonic Orchestra, is a particularly good one.

Uses for it are suggested in Section 4: the opening provides music for such things as exploration of caves, or other planets, whilst the rest can be built up into dance drama. This version also includes the 'Tarentalla' from *La Boutique Fantasque*, which can be used as an early experiment in pure dance.

The Love of Three Oranges—PROKOFIEV

Much of this is useful, particularly the 'Marche', which provides a better background for some kinds of rhythmic movement than *The Syncopated Clock*. Two cheap versions are available—(i) with *Lieutenant Kijé* (used as background music in the film *The Horse's Mouth*) (Decca ACL 159), or (ii) with the *Nutcracker Suite* (MFP 2047)—and the choice depends upon the coupling that you would find most useful.

Maria Elena—LOS INDIOS TABAJARAS (RCA 1365)

Useful for anything in slow motion.

If more money is available, the following records are all worth considering in some way or another.
Music for 'warm-up': this kind of music is used so frequently, that a limited selection soon becomes hackneyed. It can be difficult to find exactly the right material. Possibilities are:

Swingin' Safari—BERT KAMPFERT (Polydor 46 384)

Jimmy Smith's Greatest Hits (VLP 9164)

The Hit Version of Zorba's Dance (plus other tracks) (DRL 50010)

Live in Las Vegas—SANDY NELSON (LBY 3035)

Many HERB ALPERT recordings, e.g. 'Spanish Flea', 'Down Cherry Street', 'Mexican Shuffle', etc.

Music for dance, drama, mood, atmosphere, etc:
Firebird, Children's Games and *Mother Goose Suite* (HMV XLP 30067)

Music For Strings, Percussion and Celesta The Miraculous Mandarin—BARTOK (Decca LXT 6111)

Concerto for Orchestra—BARTOK (Supraphon SUA 10515)

Carnival of Animals—SAINT-SAËNS (MFP 2041)

Divertissement—IBERT (MFP 2041)

Musical Gems of the 20th Century—MILHAUD (Supraphon SUA 10479)

Useful for the inclusion of 'La Création du Monde'.

Romeo and Juliet—PROKOFIEV (Supraphon SUA 10104)

Billy the Kid and *Rodeo*—COPELAND (BRG 72411)

Chazz—THE CHARLIE MINGUS QUINTET (LAE 543)

Especially a track called 'Percussion Discussion'.

Hary Janos—KODALY (MFP 2042)

Music of India—RAVI SHANKAR (HMV ALP 1665)

Le Coq D'Or—RIMSKI KORSAKOV (Decca ACL 43)

Mammoth Fair Organ (Decca ACL 1124)

Façade—WALTON (Decca ACL 219)

The Rite of Spring—STRAVINSKY (Supraphon SUA 10487)

Some record companies are now only issuing stereophonic recordings, and have deleted monophonic versions from their catalogues. To avoid confusion, 'mono' numbers have been quoted throughout this section. Record dealers will give information on current stereo equivalents where necessary.

NOTE: Before contemplating the purchase of stereo records, read the notes under *Buying new equipment*, page 148.

PERCUSSION INSTRUMENTS

Some percussion instruments are essential. If you have the chance of buying these, rather than 'borrowing' them from the music department, then it is worth investing in good

K

quality instruments from a specialist supplier. The usual type provided for school use are often small and give a poor 'thin' sound. Cheap cymbals may even bend or curl back at the edges.

Your first need will be for a drum of some sort. A side-drum can be used quite successfully, and often there will be one about in the school, but if you are buying one a good tambour and striker will be more convenient because it is less cumbersome. Select one of about 15 inches diameter, preferably in a case in order to avoid damage.

A pair of cymbals will be almost as valuable as a tambour. Choose a good quality pair of about 14 inches diameter. Try to acquire or improvise a felt striker; it will enable you to hit one cymbal alone and achieve a softer 'gong' effect than is possible by simply clashing the pair together.

Apart from these it is well worth collecting and improvising a selection of various sound-making devices. Those that you could buy next include a tambourine, Chinese blocks and Indian bells. The important thing is to have a variety of sounds available. Do not scorn the possibilities of dried peas in an old cocoa tin.

GRAMOPHONES

Although the drama teacher can probably manage with almost any gramophone, a machine designed especially for the job will be of far more use. Such machines do exist and usually include some, if not all, of the following features:

1. *External loudspeaker*. A large loudspeaker set apart from the gramophone itself has several advantages. It usually improves the sound quality. It allows the sound source to

be sited to give the best spread of sound, i.e., high on a wall midway down the hall. It is easier to adjust the volume if the speaker is well away from the controls.

2. *Twin single-playing turntables.* An autochange unit is a nuisance as the complicated switching and additional paraphernalia are likely to hinder speedy operation. Twin turntables with separate volume controls are invaluable. They allow cross fading of two records; they allow another record to be set up while one is playing, and, if you are using records of different speeds, avoid the delay caused by the need to make stylus and speed changes.

3. *Stop switches.* Even single-playing turntables usually have some kind of automatic stopping mechanism which cuts in at the end of a record. This is a major problem as the mechanism invariably cuts in if you attempt to pick out an extract near the centre of the record, particularly with 45 r.p.m.s. They are also noisy if the volume control is up when they are functioning. Disconnecting the automatic stopping mechanism is not difficult, and it can easily be replaced by a simple toggle switch (make sure that this is muted). The pick-up can then be placed on the appropriate spot on the record before the turntable is started.

4. *Alternative inputs.* You will often find it useful to be able to play a tape recorder or use a microphone through the gramophone amplifier and speaker. To facilitate this, appropriate input sockets must be fitted, but for maximum versatility ensure that each input has a separate volume control, as it may be necessary to have the microphone at a higher volume level than a tape recording that is playing at the same time.

5. *Output.* Enough volume is needed to fill the hall. Volume is like horse-power; it feels and sounds sweeter when not pushed to the limit, so be generous and have more than you think you will need. In audio terms an output of about 12 watts is advisable.

Modifications to existing equipment

If you inherit or are provided with the standard 'schools' model gramophone, the average school science department should be able to modify it to meet at least some of the above requirements. For example:

An autochange unit could be converted to a single-playing one.
The automatic stop could be replaced with a switch.
External loudspeaker connections could be fitted.

These suggestions are not just gimmicks but are definite aids to easier and more efficient drama teaching.

Buying new equipment

The larger suppliers of school audio equipment do list machines which fulfil some of these requirements, but generally they tend to lack flexibility and really good sound quality.

The ideal answer, if the Authority allows it, is to have a machine built to your own requirements.

Increasingly, manufacturers are producing only stereo equipment and recordings. For a true stereo effect, the position of the listeners in relation to the loudspeaker is critical. Such a situation is impossible to achieve in drama sessions where people will be continuously moving about whilst records are playing. Stereo, therefore, has no particular advantage in these circumstances, and may in some situations be a nuisance.

If you are contemplating the purchase of mono equipment for the sake of economy, or are using existing mono, it is important to ensure that it is adapted for the playing of any stereo records that you may have to buy. These will otherwise be quickly spoilt and become unusable. The playing of stereo records on a mono gramophone simply involves the replacement of the mono cartridge in the pickup head by one designed for stereo. This can be done quite cheaply, and ensures the safety of your stereo records—it will not affect the machine's ability to play mono records. All the records you play, of course, will only be reproduced monophonically.

TAPE RECORDERS

A tape recorder is desirable but not essential. Its use in normal drama lessons is limited, as your recorded music may have to be selected from several tapes, and it is hardly practicable to hold up the lesson while tapes are changed or run backwards and forwards to find the part you need. Records are far more convenient. The use of the tape recorder in 'radio work' is dealt with very fully in books devoted especially to the subject, such as *Broadcasting with Children* by Kenneth Methold (U.L.P.). This book also includes a useful section on tape recording equipment and microphones.

ROSTRUM BLOCKS

Day-to-day drama work will be greatly enhanced if the children have at their disposal a selection of portable rostrum blocks. They will add interest and variety to the floor space by providing different levels. If the school cannot afford to buy or make them it is well worthwhile considering the possibility of improvising blocks from such things as old, suitably cut-down tables, etc.

If you are buying there is a choice of several specially made sets of blocks some of which fit neatly and compactly into a small space. They have been designed for use by certain education authorities, and usually bear the name of the authority (the 'Essex' blocks). The disadvantages, however, are that they are either too small to be valuable, or so massive and solid that children have difficulty in moving them.

By far the best way is to make them yourself, or have them made to your own specifications. If you do this, decide upon a standard size, and make the other of such a size that they can all be used together easily. A good standard size is 6′ × 3′ × 1′ (perhaps three or four of these). Add to these five or six blocks 3′ × 3′ × 1′ and a few 3′ × 1′ 6″ × 6″, and you will have a useful selection.

All blocks should be made strongly enough to stand up to hard usage, but light enough for children to move without undue difficulty. It is worth considering holes in the sides of the larger blocks to facilitate carrying, and perhaps some form of rubber protection on the underside to save the floor. The best finish is distemper or emulsion paint. This provides a surface that responds well to stage lighting, can easily be changed or renewed, and reduces to a minimum the chances of slipping.

SCRIPTED PLAYS

The drama teacher should always ensure that the play he chooses is going to make a positive contribution to the drama work throughout the school. The following points should be borne in mind:

1. A scripted play is not the end-product of a drama course in schools; it is merely one aspect of it. The course is aimed at personal development rather than a training for the stage.
2. The selected play should not only fulfil the obvious need for a clear plot, simple dialogue and a large cast, but should also provide opportunities for the children to use their creative powers, to improvise within the framework of the text (see also Section 7). Brian Way's *Pinocchio* is an excellent example.
3. When asking younger children to take part in formal productions there are two main dangers: they are likely to become artificial and stilted, thereby losing much of the value of their previous drama work, and they may be subjected to the confusing experience of having an adult audience find them 'quaint' and laughing in places where the children see no humour at all. To avoid the latter danger, as Peter Slade observes, the Nativity play and the Passion are the 'safest' in that audiences know, as it were, how to behave on these occasions.

The creating of plays from good stories, under the leadership of the teacher (see block 17, page 106), is generally the best way. Instead of starting with a story the teacher can sometimes begin with a generally suitable play which can be simplified and adapted to meet the needs of the children, as for example *The Blue Bird* by Maeterlinck.

Younger seniors

As has already been observed, with this age group it is more appropriate to think in terms of improvisation and adaptation rather than of the ready-made play. However, some authors have written plays of quality suitable for acting by younger seniors. Attention should be called to the work of Brian Way, particularly *The Storytellers* in his book *Three Plays for the Open Stage*, and also to *The Tinder Box* and other plays by Nicholas Stuart Gray.

Older seniors

The following list contains suggestions of plays for older seniors. The starred titles denote plays that with imaginative adaptation might be suitable for younger seniors.

*The Pied Piper—various versions.
*The Snow Queen—MAGITO and WEIL.
*The Tinder Box—NICHOLAS STUART GRAY.
*The Storytellers—BRIAN WAY.
　Pinocchio—BRIAN WAY.
　The Dark Tower⎱ both in LOUIS MACNEICE's book *The Dark*
　The Nosebag　⎰　*Tower.*
　The Pardoner's Tale—JAMES BRIDIE.
**Toad of Toad Hall*—A. A. MILNE.
　1066 and All That—SELLAR and YEATMAN.

The Rose and the Ring—THACKERAY.

The Blue Bird—MAETERLINCK.

Columbus—LOUIS MACNEICE.

Columbus Sails—MAISIE COBBY (to be found in Book IV of *Calling all Playmakers*). This book also provides useful material for adaptation and suggests ways in which it might be approached.

Richard of Bordeaux—GORDON DAVIOT.

Jonah and the Whale—BRIDIE.

Tobias and the Angel—BRIDIE.

Noah—ANDRÉ OBEY.

The True Mystery of the Passion—ARNOUL GREBAN, translated by JAMES KIRKUP.

The Boy with a Cart—CHRISTOPHER FRY (some of the longer speeches will probably need cutting).

The First Born—CHRISTOPHER FRY.

Green Pastures—MARC CONNELLY.

Little plays of St. Francis LAURENCE HOUSMAN.

A Man Dies—MARVIN and HOOPER.

St. George and the Dragon.

The Wakefield Cycle—edited and slightly modernised by MARTIAL ROSE.

The York Cycle—edited and slightly modernised by J. S. PURVIS.

The Chester Cycle—selected and slightly modernised by MAURICE HUSSEY.

Three Medieval Plays—edited by JOHN ALLEN.

The Chester Deluge Play
The Townley Plays (Wakefield)   available in various editions and collections.
The Second Shepherds' Play

The Dumb Wife of Cheapside—translated by ASHLEY DUKES.
The Shoemaker's Holiday—THOMAS DEKKER.
Our Town—THORNTON WILDER.
Lady Precious Stream—S. I. HSIUNG.
The Bespoke Overcoat—WOLF MANKOWITZ.
Round the World in Eighty Days—adapted from JULES VERNE's book by MONTAGU SLATER.
Three Comedies—LUDVIG HOLBERG.

The difficulty of drawing an exact line between what is and what is not practicable will be apparent from perusal of the above list. As one approaches work suitable for the sixth forms of grammar schools the bounds become very wide. The main limiting factor is that although adolescents are intellectually capable of understanding almost any play, there are experiences for which, however clever, they are not emotionally ready. While on the one hand grammar schools have been known to make a success of Miller's *The Crucible*, one wonders whether plays based upon disillusionment, such as Strindberg's *The Father*, T. Williams's *Camino Real* or Ibsen's *The Ghosts*, could be performed with any real insight. Clever children can be coached to reproduce practically anything; but this misses the whole point—acting of any value, whether to actor or to audience, must come from within and not be imposed from without. (The fact that many audiences and some critics cannot distinguish between the two kinds of acting makes no difference to the artistic and educational principles involved.) For these reasons the selected play should be based on experiences into which the sixth-former has emotional insight. It follows from this that the better the quality of the play the more likely it is to have a basis of genuine and broad humanity which is likely to elicit an intuitive and sincere response from all those who have reached the verge of adulthood. The worst possible choice will be the slick 'West End success', which whiles away an evening.

The value of Shakespeare is already well understood, and to this should be added a fuller use of medieval drama, the greatness of which becomes more apparent once one escapes from preoccupation with the 'picture frame' stage and the 'well-made play'. The double bill of *Everyman* and Brecht's *The Trial of Lucullus*, staged by one grammar school, must have made an exciting evening. *Everyman* is well known, but the earlier 'mystery' texts abound in a vividness and reality which would stimulate any group led by an imaginative producer. For most audiences some modernisation of the language is probably inevitable, although this should be kept to the absolute minimum.

A separate booklet would be required to list all the plays that could be brought within the scope of grammar school productions. The following titles are intended only to illustrate and to stimulate ideas about what might be done.

Everyman and Medieval Miracle Plays—edited by A. C.
   CAWLEY, contains 14 selected plays from all the Cycles.
The Interlude of Youth—
   (See also medieval plays listed under 'older seniors'.)
The Government Inspector—NIKOLAI GOGOL.
The Trial of Lucullus—BRECHT.
The Lark—JEAN ANOUILH.
Murder in the Cathedral—T. S. ELIOT.
The Crucible—ARTHUR MILLER.

The Rape of the Locks—MENANDER.

The Misanthrope—MOLIÈRE.

Doctor Faustus—MARLOWE.

The Zeal of Thy House—DOROTHY L. SAYERS.

A Man for all Seasons—ROBERT BOLT.

Blood Wedding—F. G. LORCA.

A Servant of Two Masters—CARLO GOLDONI, translated by EDWARD DENT.

Ralph Roister Doister—NICOLAS UDALL
Gammer Gurton's Needle—ANONYMOUS } World Classics: *Five Pre-Shakespearian Comedies.*

Androcles and the Lion—G. B. SHAW.

The Mock Doctor—HENRY FIELDING (adapted from MOLIÈRE).

Romanoff and Juliet—PETER USTINOV.

The Lady's not for Burning—CHRISTOPHER FRY.

Saint Joan—G. B. SHAW.

The Cradle Song—GREGORIO SIERRA, translated by JOHN UNDERHILL. Mainly for girls.

The Satire of the Three Estates—SIR DAVID LINDSAY.

Ambrose Applejohn's Adventure—WALTER HACKETT.

The range already indicated is enormous, and a group which feels capable of tackling *Hamlet* need not feel debarred from attempting such plays as *Peer Gynt* or *Brand* (MICHAEL MEYER'S translation).

Index